DISPLAY &
VISUAL
MERCHANDISING

A
RETAIL
ACTION
GUIDE

NUMBER 2

DISPLAY &
VISUAL
MERCHANDISING

Ken White and Frank White, ISP

ST. FRANCIS PRESS, WESTWOOD, NJ

ISBN   1-884951-05-8

First published in 1996

Library of Congress Cataloging in Publication Data

White, Ken, Display & Visual Merchandising, with Frank White

1. Display of Merchandising - Handbooks, manuals, etc.   2. Merchandising - Handbooks, manuals, etc.   I. White, Frank II. Title: Display & Visual Merchandising

This publication is designed to provide accurate and authoritative information in regard to the subject matter covered. It is sold with the understanding that the author and the publisher are not engaged in rendering legal, accounting or related services.

"Retail Action Guide" © Series are published by St. Francis Press. Its Trademark, consisting of the words "Retail Action Guide" © is registered in the U.S. Patent and Trademark Office and in other countries. Marca Registrada. Retail Action Guide ©, St. Francis Press, 7 James St., Westwood, NJ 07675.

Printed in Hong Kong.

"Retail Action Guide" © Series books are available at special discounts when purchased in bulk for premiums and sales promotions as well as for fund-raising or educational use. Special editions or book excerpts can also be created to specification. For details, contact the Special Sales Director at 201-664-5664 or write: Sales Director, St. Francis Press, 7 James St., Westwood, NJ 07675

Contents

Getting Down to Cases 11; Leveraging DVM in Your Store 11; Storefront
Show Windows 12; Philosophy of Show Window Design 13; Open-Back vs
Closed-Back Show Windows 13; Combination Open and Closed-Back
Show Windows 13; Imperative Interior Displays 16; Feature Areas 16;
New-Arrival Table and Wall Displays 16; New, "New-Arrival" Display
 Concepts 16; Sale and Theme Tables 16; Aisle Merchandisers, End-Caps,
and T-Walls 17; Focal Points 20; Column and Ledge Displays 20;
POS/Cash Wrap and Information Desk Merchandising 20; Glass Interior
Show Windows and Display Showcases 20; Vestibules 20

Materials 25; Window Backings 25; Ribbons and Streamers 27;
Bamboo Blinds, Venetian Blinds, and Roller Shades 28; Foam Core and
Gator Board 33; Sale and Theme 34; Lattice Panels and Screens 34;
Folding Screens 36; Display Cubes, Pedestals, and Chairs 36;
The Display Calendar 38; When to Change Window Displays 39;
Preparing to Display Merchandise 39; Advance Preparation 42;
Show Time 42; Display Tools 43

Image by Choice 45; Permanent Image-Building Elements 45; Changeable
Image-Building Elements 46; Designing for Mood and Appeal 48;
Emotional Appeal 48; Creating the Mood 48; Creating Themes 48;
Choosing the Right Theme 49; No Mood At All 51; Timing Mood Displays
and Themes 53; Symmetrical Balance 53; Asymmetrical Balance 54;
Interior Display 55

1 Title page illustration: ***The simple and effective use of red, white, and blue banners*** *at the top of this patriotic theme window display is balanced with draped fabric hung over display steps to form the shape of an invisible triangle. The color form and staging were used to set the mood for introducing the title, "Civil War." Gold leaf lettering was applied to the inside of open-faced glass windows....would be good to know who the display designer really was.* Scribner, New York, N.Y.

ALSO BY KEN WHITE

Bookstore Planning & Design

Campus Convenience Store Planning Manual

Independent Bookstore Planning & Design

Espresso, Cappuccino, and Caffé Latté Coffeehouses and Cafe's, etc.
with Frank White

HOW TO USE THIS GUIDE

The symbols alongside a title or within
the text itself provide cross-references
to subject matter, photo illustrations, or
the use of a product/DVM technique.

▲   PHOTO ILLUSTRATION

◆   FURTHER DISCUSSION OF THE SUBJECT

Preface and Acknowledgments

Now that you have a store to own or manage and the assortment of books and merchandise that go into it, a major issue is how to arrange and present the merchandise to its best advantage. The presentation of merchandise requires space in display show windows and at strategic locations throughout the store. Display tables, pedestals, and store fixtures are needed to merchandise the assortments the store intends to sell. In this book we will look at the elements and techniques to combine to create a visual merchandising strategy throughout the store. It is a strategy over which you have complete control. The cost to implement display and visual merchandising ideas can be as much or as little as you choose to spend.

Display and visual merchandising, or DVM as we call it, is one of the best tools retailers can use to grow their businesses. To be skilled in the proper use of display and visual merchandising concepts and techniques in today's economy is to wield a double-edged sword. DVM can be the force to make books and merchandise fly.

Independent bookstores and specialty shops of all types face increasing competition from superstores, mega stores, mail and television catalogues, and mass merchandise discount stores. In today's fiercely competitive marketplace, DVM can be the difference between growing or joining the ranks of stores that are no more.

Ask ten retailers to define display and visual merchandising and you will hear ten or more complicated and diverse explanations. The reason is that there is no single right way. Its ultimate *raison d'être,* though, is to orchestrate the presentation and stimulate the sale of books and merchandise offered by the store–with flair–but with a reflection of what the store stands for in the community and for the audience it seeks to attract.

This book is aimed at students and those who practice DVM. Experienced display people and visual merchandising staff can use this book to brush up on the basics. The book is a clear, concise guide divided into two parts. Part 1 deals with DVM, strategy, concepts, materials, and tools. In part 2 the focus is how to apply these merchandising ideas in retail stores.

Our thanks to the achievers who opened their stores to us to take hundreds of photographs, and who were without exception cooperative and hospitable.

Thanks also to Andy and JoAnn for endless hours of patiently helping to organize and present this new Retail Action Guide.

If you are a business owner or hold a managerial position with a large publishing or retail organization, whether you handle the display and visual merchandising yourself or direct a staff of experts, this Retail Action Guide is for you.

Let's get going!

Ken White and Frank White
Westwood, NJ – 1995

Part 1

DVM: Display and Visual Merchandising

1

The starting point for this book is to define "display and visual merchandising" (DVM). DVM is the total impact of display, marketing, advertising, and publicity activities necessary for a retail business to succeed in a particular community. DVM brings into view, shows, puts in plain light, exhibits, demonstrates, and presents merchandise and services to customers in a retail setting.

The visual part of DVM deals with the external and internal look and feel of the display; the composition, grouping, and arrangement of merchandise; and the image, tone, atmosphere, and visual character of the retail store.

More explicitly, visual merchandising is the technical process of displaying products in a show window to entice customers to stop, view the display, want to see more of the store, and enter to the promise of an enjoyable shopping experience. From the retailer's point of view, the first purpose of DVM is to help generate sales volume and to produce a profit for the business. The second and equally important purpose is to create and support a positive store image.

Getting Down to Cases

DVM is actively pursued as an essential part of all successful retail sales and promotion planning in the United Kingdom, Europe, Japan, the Pacific Rim, Canada, and the United States. It is an important activity for all retail businesses.

The types of DVM activity for a particular merchandising promotion determines the best location in the promotion plan for the display of a particular item. DVM plans need not be complex and costly, but they need to be organized. Simple, inexpensive, and results-oriented DVM techniques are essential for every size store. It is critical for stores with modest resources that are "looking for an edge."

Leveraging DVM in Your Store

Because the size, shape, and mission of each retail business varies so widely, we have divided the typical DVM program into seven feature areas, each a direct element of merchandising activity. Each activity can take place at a different location outside and inside the store, often at the same time. Let's start by looking at each of the seven DVM elements and why each is important.

2 Left: *The typical pedestrian takes less than seven seconds to pass an average show window. Moveable curb sign is designed to catch the eye of the passerby.* WORDSWORTH ABRIDGED, Cambridge, Mass.

3 Right: *Classical and neoclassical store front elements* combined to create an upscale image for Bollingers Books, Oklahoma City, Okla.
4 Below R: *Two-story shop front* comes alive at night on the Walkplatz. Kaiser Buchhandlung, Munich, Ger.
5 Below L: *Combination high open and low, closed-back windows* facing Fifth Avenue. Scribner, New York, N.Y.

Storefront
Show Windows

The foremost role of the show window display is to slow walk-by traffic and motivate customers to enter the store. Just as important, show window DVM efforts are intended to show, inform, and support the image of the store.

The shop front and show window together give shoppers their first impression of the store; it's specialty, selection, price, service, and market position; and it's image.

Show window displays are the universal means employed by small stores to present their selections. It is the primary means to tell the story of their "unique" book selections, category mix, and product offering. Show windows provide the retailer with complete control over what customers will see in the display. They are critical to the success of small and medium-size stores in urban and strip malls.

Attitudes toward show window displays vary. Because they are generally set back from pedestrian traffic and located in parking lots, few large superstores use theme show window displays. Superstores depend on massive structure, advertising, and exterior signing to attract and stop traffic. New energy-conscious superstores located in the Sunbelt regions of the United

Table 1: The Seven Elements of DVM	
1. Storefront show windows	5. Focal points; columns and ledges
2. New-arrival table and wall displays	6. POS/cash wrap and information desk merchandising
3. Sale and theme tables	7. High and low-glass display showcases
4. Aisle merchandisers, end-caps, and T-walls	

States bypass show windows altogether to reduce operating expenses. Elsewhere, windows in superstores are made as large as practical and merchandising energies are focused on interior DVM ▲53.

Show windows are the most important DVM tool at a store's disposal. There is virtually an unlimited variety of architectural designs for show window arrangements ▲73. Show windows are found in every city. They face indoor and outdoor arcades, shopping centers, lobbies, and halls. Traditional and contemporary shop fronts with one or more single or multistory show windows stand comfortably, as we shall see, with their neighbors facing streets, plazas, and car parks ▲59.

Philosophy of Show Window Design

One of the first questions the owner, store designer, and DVM specialist must consider when new stores are built or remodeled is whether the show windows are to have open or closed backs. In general, small stores are designed with open-back windows and larger stores with combination open and closed-back windows ▲1, 5. Traditional storefronts usually have one or two show windows separated by an entrance into the store.

Open-Back vs Closed-Back Show Windows

The majority of bookstore owners who retain us to design stores for them in the United States and overseas prefer open-back window displays. Among the advantages are that shoppers can see right through the window to the inside of the store interior ▲5. The unified display that results from combining the store front with the interior is a great advantage. Open-back windows offer the possibility of creating a friendly, informal atmosphere that draws people inside. They also stand out from the crowd, particularly at night. Inexpensive props and easily moved backings can be used in open-back windows to create an endless variety of interesting themes.

Closed-back windows can be planned as a stage in which the display person can use all the resources of window trimmings and stagecraft. Besides the opportunities it offers for drama in display, the closed-back window allows more variety in a range of presentations ▲85. The typical closed-back show window has a floor and ceiling, three opaque walls, and a small access door at either end or in the back. The privacy offered by the closed-back window may be suitable for many stores.

Combination Open and Closed-Back Show Windows ◆12

Because the advantages of both the open and closed-back window are so pronounced, the two basic types of show windows are often combined into a single storefront design. The design of combination storefronts has two objectives. The first is to add wall shelving against the closed-back of the window to display more book titles. The second purpose is to conceal building structural and mechanical support systems. Combination versions of open/closed show window storefronts can often be seen in buildings remodeled for retailing ▲5.

6 Above: *Imaginative single-title round sale table display.* *Customers can pick up a book without destroying the display.* STACEY'S, San Francisco, Calif. 7 Below L: *Every gondola end is fully merchandised* *with books and cards.* WORDSWORTH, Cambridge, Mass. 8 Below R: *New arrival whale display* *w/step base and face out shelves with displays on four sides.* UNIVERSITY BOOKSTORE, Madison, Wisc.

9 Above: *New arrival table* and store directory. DILLON'S, London, U.K.

10 Right and 11 Bottom R: *New arrival hardbound fiction wall display. Selected books are pulled out* to support more copies and pack more capacity onto the shelves. WORDSWORTH, Cambridge, Mass.

12 Below: *Category signage on ends of T-wall gondolas is "keyed" to a store directory to help customers find the books they want. Face out dumps and end-caps emphasize the DVM promotional value of the displays.* Bollingers Books, Oklahoma City, Okla.

Imperative Interior Displays

Good interior presentations leave no question in the shoppers' minds of what store they are in or exactly what the store is selling. The degree to which the seven crucial DVM elements (table 1) are emphasized directly depends on the size of the store and the goal of its marketing plan. The degree to which interior DVM techniques are pursued varies dramatically from store to store. Yet the one question booksellers most frequently ask is, "Where do I build interior displays in the store?" Table 1 describes the natural locations where customers expect to find DVM displays inside any store. Plans for most new stores usually overlook the need to provide quality DVM features and locations. General architects and store-fixture manufacturers are primarily concerned with architectural aesthetics and marketing store fixtures so they often leave DVM details, perhaps rightfully, for you, the owner-manager, to handle. At Ken White Associates, as a matter of course, we talk it through with the owner and make provision for DVM presentations in all the stores our firm designs. The sales that result from thoughtful preplanning and incorporating DVM requirements confirm the wisdom of providing DVM presentations inside the store.

Feature Areas

Six of the seven feature areas of DVM (table 1) are located inside the store. Each element provides an introduction and high-lights an offer of book, merchandise, or services. Each element has an impact on the customers, category impact, price/value, seasonal impact, or promotional impact. Price/value impact means highlighting bargains such as, "Our Everyday Low Price," "Books for a Buck," and so forth. Promotional impact means items on sale or on clearance.

New-Arrival Table and Wall Displays ◆99

The first display to greet customers inside the store should be the new-arrival tables stacked with recently released books, music, or sidelines. This is imperative to create a good first impression.

Customers usually respond to strategically placed new-arrival displays. People will stop at displays that are highly visible, accessible, signed, organized, and maintained. Book titles displayed face out, raised up, and signed with a well-written, peppy, make-them-want-to-buy message, are the kind of visual displays that stops customer traffic and sells books and sidelines. Tables for new-arrival displays are found in a variety of rectangular, round ▲6, or hexagonal shapes. Flat-top table displays built up with risers, cubes, stacker boxes ◆34, and better yet, signed with banners, account for significant sales ▲17.

The customer entering a long, narrow bookstore with limited floor space should be greeted by a first-rate, new-arrival display located in a high wall display fixture ▲10. New-arrival wall displays in the right situation have proven to be very successful.

New, "New-Arrival" Display Concepts

The customer entering a new superstore may encounter a "new-arrival whale." Whales are versatile versions of step gondola selling fixtures ▲8. Whales are favored by independent and chain superstores because they are capable of holding "a whale of a lot of books." The fact that whales can be easily converted to market sale books ▲147, large format art or children's books ▲150, calendars, stationery, back-to-school promotions, and other sidelines and promotions adds to their value ◆102.

Sale and Theme Tables ◆99

Shoppers flowing through a store and encountering sale and theme tables become curious about the merchandise. These sales fixtures provide a location and platform for displays that convert wanderers and browsers into customers ▲130. Sale and theme tables are one of the most functional display tools DVM people have at their disposal. One or more sale tables can be assembled to present single title or mixed-subject presentations of sale books, remainders, specialty sidelines, or calendars. Casters add flexibility by making it easy to move and rearrange particular theme requirements. Moving tables to create room for discussion groups, demonstrations, readings, story telling, author signing, or other in-store events allows the flexibility needed in today's sales' environment ◆116.

Aisle Merchandisers, End-Caps, and T-Walls

Aisle merchandisers, end-caps, and directional signage located at the ends of gondolas invite the customer deeper into the store ▲7, 20, 47. Aisle merchandisers help to generate sales by displaying a wide variety of specialty and backlist books and sidelines. With good store fixture equipment and lots of imagination, an endless variety of impulse items can be successfully merchandised at these important locations.

The design of end-caps has changed from flat panels (against which books were piled on stacker boxes) to slatwall ends (with plastic tray and waterfall type inserts and holders) to end-cap designs (with tables and risers and stands) that present multiple tiers of display. The styling of these end-cap tables and risers may be eclectic or follow the design of the store interior. Seasonal themes at end-caps can be reinforced with posters, signs, and props ◆84.

High T-wall fixturing is used to "boutique" perimeter sales departments. T-walls also add high-wall book capacity in the store ▲110. T-walls are an ideal tool for creating merchandise separation. They are also used to create focus departments. T-walls create separate shops within the store that prevent visual conflict with adjacent merchandise. T-walls justify a visual change of color, style of fixture, graphics, or props. They can be used to create a unique, "shop within a shop," that is separate but compatible with the image of the store.

13 Above: **High glass display cases** *can also be used as space builders to create specialty departments.* Academy Bookstore, U.S. Naval Academy, Annapolis, Md.

14 Below: **End-cap of island type cashier station** *carries a strong image message. It lets the customer know where they are and what to expect from the store.* Sam Goody's, Los Angeles, Calif.

Sign with announcement of the theme

Sign holder with long legs

Cube/stacker box to raise the sign and offer

Face out display in slatwall acrylic holder

Gifts

Sign visible from two directions

Mixed titles on risers and easels

Table top Pick N' Take stacks

Face up title display on easels

15 Above: *Hexagon theme table merchandised with gift books.* B&N, New York, N.Y.
16 Below: *New-arrival (release) music table.* B&N, New York, N.Y.

Customers expect to find full, and well-merchandised, new-arrival and theme tables in the front of small stores, and at the entrance of major theme areas in large stores.

Sign: Eye level announcement offer

Open face display

NEW RELEASES ON SALE

Offer: two high

Quantity Pick N' Take merchandise riser

Open table base

17 Above: **Focal point** *travel theme merchandising features maps, posters, globes on stacker boxes, travel guides, and publisher POS material.* 18 Right: **POS cash wrap** *desk merchandised with prerecorded tapes, and bookmarks.* Both: Bollingers Books, Oklahoma City, Okla.

Focal Points

The best selling locations in the store are usually found at the intersection of main customer aisles. In stores with limited space, focal points are found on the ends of T-walls, end-caps, and gondolas ▲19. Focal points are key locations where displayed items will sell. Displays designed for these locations are intended to present new products and innovative ideas. They are intended to stimulate interest in the merchandise. The displays seem to shout, "Hey, look at me! I want to be picked up." Focal points along aisles create a fresh merchandising "look" and a unified appeal throughout the store ▲12.

Column and Ledge Displays

For all practical purposes, shelves found on the top of graphic ledges, wall cases, T-walls, and columns are natural locations to create additional display spaces, usually above the shelving surrounding it. End-cap merchandisers can be placed against flat, wide columns that can be enclosed with slatwall when needed ▲181. Because columns are often enclosed to conceal electrical wiring and utilities, they are also logical locations to position listening stations ▲163, workstations, lighted signs, and display devices, that need electrical power. Ledges around the tops of gondolas and shadow boxes of varying sizes and shapes can be built into and between columns. Ledge displays on walls and around the tops of gondolas can become potent, easy to use display points ▲21.

POS/Cash Wrap and Information Desk Merchandising

As the customers complete their shopping in the store and move to the cash-wrap/checkout counter, then point-of-purchase display and other forms of merchandising take over. The cash wrap is the place to feature distinctive seasonal book titles and accessories that ask: "Did you see this?" This is the place where add-on sales take place. It is the spot to market new and noteworthy items, such as small books, magnifiers, bookmarks, notes, and magazines. Customers like to browse through and buy promotionally priced, prerecorded music audio tapes at this location ▲18, 22, 24.

The cash-wrap/information service desk is also the place where many stores merchandise gift certificates, take and fulfill special orders, gift wrap purchases, send and receive faxes, and market a long list of other speciality services. This is the place to dispense store promotion material, store maps, service directories, book club cards, and business cards. It is also the place to feature new-arrival, mass-market titles that relate to the special focus of the store.

Glass Interior Show Windows and Display Showcases

DVM managers enjoy saying to new staff members, "Think of showcases as mini show windows," and they are right. Glass showcases are also thought of as inside image-building show windows. They are available in a variety of sizes and designs. Showcases are frequently combined with cash wrap stations ▲23, 40. The value of showcases lies in their unique ability to direct attention to small and valuable articles that might get lost in a large show window or disappear from an open counter top. Better books, gifts, and jewelry can take on an appealing mark of distinction when properly displayed in showcases. High-margin computer software, museum quality reproductions, jewelry ▲13, and quality merchandise such as select, rare, and limited edition books are other products typically displayed in showcase displays located throughout the store. Tall showcases are often used in bookstores to feature rare, expensive, signed, and limited edition books ▲129, and to market quality sidelines.

Selling out of a showcase or a show window is an art, and a profitable one at that.

Vestibules

For stores entered directly from the street, vestibules are great places to create a good first impression of the store's interior. A vestibule of ample width offers both a welcome area and a year-round marketing opportunity to generate impulse sales. A poster created with the "in-store PC," listing the names of the authors who have appeared in the store over the years, is a good example of a "watch us grow" idea.

> The ends of medium and high store fixtures are more likely to be seen by customers moving through the store, than are displays shelved out of sight in a row of gondolas.

19 Above L: **New-arrival cooking table display** *with a riser that lifts books up above the table, a remainder book whale, service desk, and T-wall store fixtures that create alcoves in the background.* Bollingers Books, Oklahoma City, Okla. 20 Above R: **End-cap with Christmas theme.** *Use small table, step stool, stacker boxes, and floral theme.* 21 Below: **Plush sidelines merchandise** *on top ledge of children's book gondola.* Noodle Kidoodle, Paramus, N.J.

Point-of-sale merchandising

22 Top: **POS (point-of-sale) merchandising** *at a cash wrap.* WORDSWORTH, Cambridge, Mass.   23 Center: **Low glass display showcase with sidelines.** Atlanta, Ga.
24 Below: **Mass step end-cap** *at checkout type cash wrap.*
BOOKS-A-MILLION, Daytona Beach, Fla.

Large vestibules are locations where people can wait out of the way of foot traffic going in and out of the store and be protected from bad weather at the same time. Vestibules are places where bikes are parked or where people can wait for the bus. As much a part of the interior as the exterior, the well-designed, image-building vestibule induces window shoppers to enter the store.

Storefront Show Windows

New-Arrival Table and Wall Displays

Sale and Theme Tables

Aisle Merchandisers, End-Caps, and T-Walls

Focal Points: Columns and Ledges

POS/Cash Wrap and Information Desk Merchandising

Glass Interior Show Windows and Display Showcases

★ ★ ★ ★ ★

This does not constitute a full-scale review of the DVM spectrum. It does, though, cover the key merchandising activities that can have a direct impact on the success of a business. Application of good DVM techniques can make an immediate difference in sales and works well for all retail bookstores. DVM will not solve all of a store's marketing problems, but you should study the use of a display and visual merchandising approach to improve the traffic flow, sales, volume, image, and bottom line of your store.

DVM: Stuff

2

Stuff: "The basic elements or essential components of anything; the essence"
- The American Design Dictionary

There is more than a kernel of truth in the statement that it takes a lot of "stuff" to capture and carry out the spirit of a DVM idea. When we talk about DVM stuff, we are referring to the materials, tools, products, and processes that bring the DVM vision into reality. In order to help you understand what all this stuff is and how it works, we will walk you through the beginning steps.

Remember the diamond and numbers ♦00 refer you to pages elsewhere in the guide that provide expanded information on the subject discussed. A reference such as ▲00 refers to illustrations of the subject. We have organized the information to avoid swamping you with too much detail. The information, however, is there when you need it. The first step is to accumulate some display materials and tools.

Materials

We recommend that you first obtain a portable storage bin with clear plastic trays. These are readily available from hardware stores and are handy devices to store fasteners, nails, and small hooks. Pick one that has a variety of drawer sizes and is stackable. As your inventory of "small stuff" grows, you may want to add additional storage units and you will find it more convenient if the units stack.

You will need a supply of fasteners for use in securing props and arranging the display. Buy an assortment of brads (small nails), and a variety of "s" hooks for hanging panels and signs to ceiling grids ▲33. You will also need barnacle clips that attach to the ceiling grids and sky hooks to hang signs, posters, bunting, banners, stands, plaques, props, rope, and backing materials.

Next, purchase a variety of display papers, foam core and gator board panels (more on this later), adhesives, wire, filament fish line, thread, rope, and backing materials. The first concern in the selection of display window materials and tools is to have and be able to install simple, attractive, and inexpensive backgrounds for selling ♦ table 2.

Window Backings

For the sake of simplicity, let's divide window backings into two categories. The first are movable and freestanding. The second are permanent, fixed backings of materials attached to the structure of the

25 Left: *Featured book titles are raised to eye level on the seats of three gold opera chairs in this stunning Christmas display. See page 40 for surprising facts about how the display was built.* Scribner, New York, N.Y.

building. When it comes to the selection of a window backing, the choice is wide and can be confusing. They come in all types of material, textures, colors, designs, and price ranges. When you select window backing materials, decide what you need before you spend any money. Decide what is functional and is ornamental. Golden Rule Number 1: Don't buy more than you need.

Movable backings, such as screens, draperies, blinds, and trellises, are successful in open and closed-back windows. When they are attached to the building, fixed backings become part of the permanent features of the window display. Construction is required in the installation of slatwall ▲30 and pegboard ▲26 backings built into case work, display ledges, or attached to walls. Fixed backings are usually restricted in their versatility. Because we are all susceptible to eye appeal in DVM, fixed backings that can be refreshed and perked up at minimal cost and effort are preferred.

Following is a partial list of popular movable and fixed backings that are found in a bookstore's bag of tricks:

Table 2: Partial Checklist of Popular Show Window Backing Materials

Wallboards

Foamcore and Gator Board
Easily worked, easily available in a variety of sizes.

Gypsum Wall Board
Known as sheetrock. It is available in fire-rated quality. It is easily worked and it can be painted and wall papered.

Homosate Board
Highly compressed wood fiber board, one side smooth, one side textured, easily worked, and used for tackable surfaces and tack boards.

Masonite
Plain and tempered, easily worked.

Particle Board
Homogeneous wood fiber board, easily shaped, stained, painted, and laminated.

Peg Board
Perforated fiber board and laminated metal facings.

Plastic Laminate
1/32"-thick laminate sheets can be cut with scissors.

Plastic Stock
Available in sheets and rolls. It is smooth, textured, and molded (cornices, pedestals).

Plywood
Traditional, contemporary, plain textured; all natural wood species and of various thicknesses.

Slatwall
Core of wood or fiberboard; variety of colors and finishes.

Finish Materials

Banners
Stock and custom banners are readily available in a variety of sizes and colors; can be saved and reused, such as grand opening banners, also used for interior and exterior signing, promotional graphic elements.

Bunting
Plain and printed striped colors available in rolls and fabricated valences.

Concrete
Portland cement can be cast into molds, troweled, molded, or textured and stained onto prepared surfaces.

Cork
Natural textured or remanufactured and compressed; used for walls, floor tile, tack boards, and plant bases.

Curtains
Available in a variety of colors, styles, and full height and cafe´ curtain designs. Ideal backing to create room settings in children's nursery, living and dining rooms, bedrooms, vignettes, and door trim.

Drapery
Ready-made items are easily available. Used in fixed and drawback arrangements to create theme settings such as Victorian, mystery, and the good life. *Caution: Drapes must be fire-retarded.*

Fabric
Synthetic, grass, natural, and mixed fiber content, available in various surface textures.

DVM: Display & Visual Merchandising

Ribbons and Streamers

No display product or category better fills the bill than ribbons and streamers, both in the foreground and the background. Ribbons are made in a wide spectrum of colors, textures, widths, and plain and multicolored designs. Ribbons are made of synthetic cloth and with fire retardant-treated paper. Colorful and exciting effects can be designed with ribbons and streamers that work well in either open- and closed-back display windows and interiors. Streamers are ribbons, strings of rope lights, rope, or any other long, narrow strip of pendant materials ▲32. Christmas, Mardi Gras, New Year's Eve, and other festive children's party themes can be created with confetti, bows, stars, and bal-

Inside tip: Floral supply companies are a good source for 100-foot long rolls of ribbon in various widths and colors and at good prices. Check them out.

Table 2 continued:

Rough textures are burlap, canvas, or denim.
Smooth: cotton, mattress ticking; plain and printed colors on synthetic fabric.
Weight: Light and heavy; used for wall covering, showcase pads, upholstery, curtains, and drapery.

Felt
Available up to 60" widths and in a variety of popular weights and colors; easily used.

Fiberglass
Fabric, flat, and corrugated sheeting.

Fishnet
Often hung as draperies, stretched over panels and loosely draped to create nautical themes.

Flags
Synthetic plastic, printed and sewn stock fabric. National, regional, and custom organizational designs available in a variety of sizes. Easy to use.

Glass
Blocks (backlight) frosted, plain, etched, textured, colored, painted, and stained surfaces. Safety laminated, heat-treated, and plain (float) qualities are available. Bought in prefabricated sizes. Easy to use.

Lattice Panels
Versatile material made of wood strips or molded panels applied to cubes, columns, and walls.

Paint
A wide variety of mat and glossy finish. Decorative colors available in water-based latex and acrylic mediums.

Paper
Available in seamless, matt, and gloss finishes. Cut sheets and rolls of smooth, textured, and corrugated surfaces. Inexpensive, paper is easily worked. Gift wrappings in a wide range of colors are available from the ABA.

Ribbons
Available in fabric and synthetic materials of varying widths, colors, and textures.

Stain
A wide variety of deep and pastel water and oil-based stains available for use on wood and wood-based products and concrete.

Stone
Natural, painted, or stained. Natural slate (1/4" thick), granite (3/16" thick), and marble tile as thin as 1/8" thick (12" x 12") are easy to use for floors and walls. Composition marble is also readily available.

Trimmings
AKA drapery trimmings. Fringe and ball fringe used to add period detail and reinforce formal settings. Hundreds of designs are available.

Vinyl Fabric
A wall covering and upholstery material available in a variety of colors, textures, and novelty designs like wood, stone, leather.

Window Roller Shades
Used to control light, as space dividers, and graphic backgrounds.

26 Above L: *Peg board wall finish in an open-back window display. Cube riser with low top glass window partition and travel posters.* Kaiser Buchhandlung, Munich, Ger. 27 Above R: *Closed-back window display on a stair.* Charlotte, N.C.

loons, all mixed with ribbons drenched in color. Celebrate anniversaries, patriotic themes, new store openings, bon voyage themes with ribbons mixed with ropes, flags, bunting ▲32, and banners. Don't hesitate to mix several colors of ribbons and textures.

Use cotton ribbon for summer themes. For winter themes use burlap, velvet, and wool textures. Then rotate back to cotton in the spring. To create important sale's day backgrounds, mix colorful ribbons with artificial flowers. For Mother's Day use frosty pink, red, and capris for Valentine's Day, and for Easter use pastels with ribbon bow knots, sprigs of artificial lilies of the valley, and pink rose buds. Ribbons can be used to make background curtains, valances, and side panels. Wrap ribbons around columns to produce maypole and swing looks. Full height ribbon panels can be tied back at the extreme ends of show windows and at divisions that make sense in the overall window presentation. Ribbons can be wrapped around the bases of feature aisle displays ▲29.

Bamboo Blinds, Venetian Blinds, and Roller Shades

Not new, but very modern in their present day use, are experiments with machine-made and hand-woven, fine, split bamboo blinds. They also provide simple, inexpensive, and interesting backings in show window display areas when that is your main objective. Bamboo blinds hung in open-back store fronts facing the morning sun provide interesting light control and patterns in a store. Individual letters, signs, and trimmings hung onto the blinds turn the backing into a

28 Above: **Narrow slatwall backing** in a closed-back shadow box type display with brick-a-brack shelves to individualize book and sideline presentation. Charlotte, N.C.

29 Above: **Slatwall columns and theme sale tables** wrapped with ribbon bows at Christmas. MEDIA PLAY, Columbus, Ohio. 30 Below: **Slatwall show window backing.** Ribbons and streamers suspended from the ceiling hold ornaments in this theme window. Shakespear & Co., New York, N.Y.

temporary focal point and billboard ▲45. The blinds can remain neutral or be painted for thematic effects.

Venetian blinds are available in an excellent range of color in dull or polished gold, silver, copper-plated, and wood finishes in 1/2" mini-thin and 1-1/2" standard widths. If needed, they can be spray painted to match or harmonize with an existing color scheme or arranged in strips of colors ▲46.

Wood blinds are also available in light and dark stain finishes to compliment wood flooring, fixtures, and furnishings inside the window and store. They are wonderful for creating natural and traditional settings. To permit the easy change of one set

of colored blinds with another, the mechanism of both 1/2" wide and 1-1/2" wide blinds are hung from the ceiling with quick change fasteners. Vertical venetian blinds are available in natural and synthetic fabric, metal, or plastic materials in a variety of lengths and widths. They too are generally hung from the ceiling. Image-building designs and messages can be screened in color onto the blinds.

The first criteria in selecting the right window backing is to add a "foil" for merchandise presentation. Common roller shades are one of the practical answers to this problem. Logos, messages, individual letters (PEACE, SALE), and slogans can be printed, screened, or applied to one or both sides of standard window shade materials ▲47. Roller shades make respectable backgrounds for books, sidelines, accessories, and small wares displayed on box buildups, pedestals, steps, platforms, etageres, and other props. Once roller brackets are mounted to the ceiling, a roller shade can be changed in less than a minute.

Generally, shades adjusted to five feet, six inches above the level of the show window permit the customer a view into the store while controlling early morning or evening sunlight penetrating the store. Adjust the blinds to admit just the right amount of light and vision needed in your situation.

One of the appeals of roller shades, is the ease with which they can be recycled. Hemmed panels of fabric cut to the width of the roller and the correct length are simply stapled onto the roller. The roller can be recycled nu-

Wreath

Ribbons

Plaid throw

Candle stick

High back bench seat

Open view into store

31 Above: *Large multi-title asymmetrical design, open-back window dressed for Christmas sales.* B&N, New York, N.Y.

High contrast, color
coordinated sign

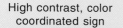

Flag

Dressed
Christmas
tree

Gift-
wrapped
packages

Tilted, multi-
titled book
display on
easels

Step
platform

Corner
bookcase

Colored
cloth floor

32 Right and opposite page: ***Easy to use props.*** *Bunting, birds, beach stuff, and things for hanging props put a little "zip" in your displays. Kid's things and natural props can add "a lot of zip" to your visual presentations. For further information, see note 1, page 127.*

Baker's Rack

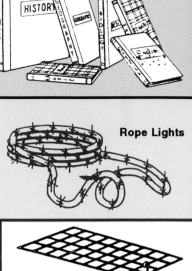

6 Piece Book Set
Fully dimensional, made of foamboard

Rope Lights

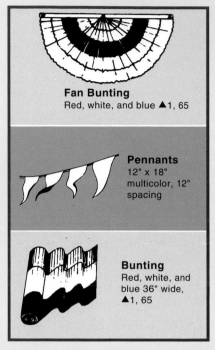

Fan Bunting
Red, white, and blue ▲1, 65

Pennants
12" x 18" multicolor, 12" spacing

Bunting
Red, white, and blue 36" wide, ▲1, 65

Flocked Trees Branches Twigs

Winterlace Trees Branches Twigs

Ceiling Grill

Magnetic Ceiling Anchors

Toggle Bolt
For hanging heavy/light grills ▲110, 134, 174

Disk/Hook-eye
Self-adhesive. Adheres to smooth surfaces

Barnacle Hook
Clips to ceiling grid

Seagull
Molded, full round

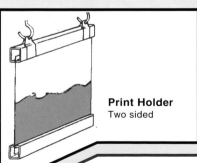

Print Holder
Two sided

Fishnet
2" mesh, 6 ' x 30 '

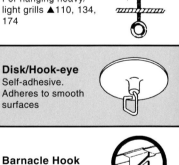

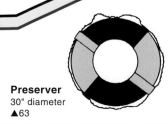

Preserver
30" diameter
▲63

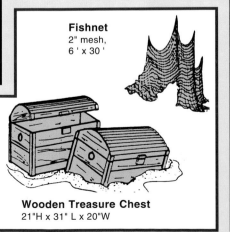

Wooden Treasure Chest
21"H x 31" L x 20"W

Steel Chain — "S" Links
Nickel, chrome, or brass ▲155

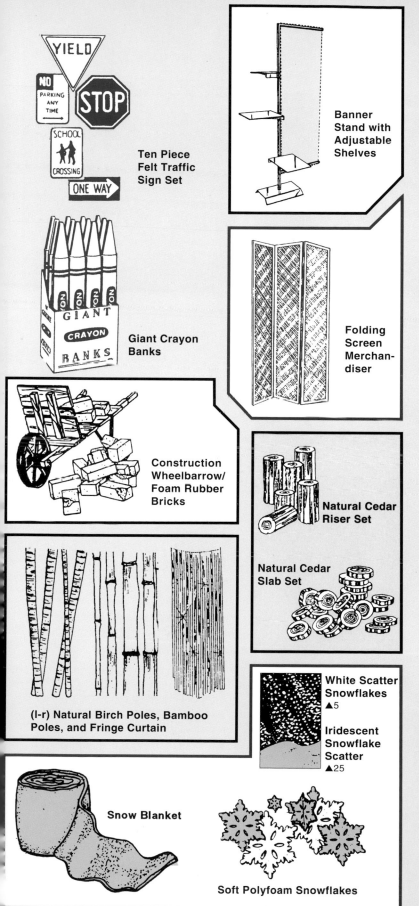

Ten Piece Felt Traffic Sign Set

Giant Crayon Banks

Banner Stand with Adjustable Shelves

Folding Screen Merchandiser

Construction Wheelbarrow/ Foam Rubber Bricks

Natural Cedar Riser Set

Natural Cedar Slab Set

(l-r) Natural Birch Poles, Bamboo Poles, and Fringe Curtain

White Scatter Snowflakes ▲5

Iridescent Snowflake Scatter ▲25

Snow Blanket

Soft Polyfoam Snowflakes

merous times in this manner.

Foam Core and Gator Board

Two of DVM's best friends, foam core and gator board, are lightweight panels of dense foam material and faced on two sides with smooth, high quality paper. There are essential differences between the materials. Foam core is white. Gator board is black, slightly more dense, and a little stronger but both boards are very stable.

Because of their stability, foam core and gator board are ideal materials for mounting advertising messages and signage. Color or black and white laser-printed messages can be generated on your PC. Mount and display promotional posters (readily available from trade publishers, but seldom used) photographs, prints, general posters, maps, directories, and other items ▲45, 56, 70.

The light weight of the boards permits them to be hung from show window ceiling grids ▲32 on hooks and tied to the floor with filament fish line to keep them straight and prevent swaying. The boards can also be mounted on vertical surfaces with double-faced foam tape or with "Fun-Tac" (children's reusable putty-like) adhesive and applied onto slatwall and other vertical surfaces. Lightweight slatwall clips can be made of aluminum strips and glued to the back of foam core and gator board panels to permit the boards to be clipped to and removed from slatwall facing materials. Floor and tabletop easels permit the boards to be displayed vertically at any point in the show

Sale and Theme Table Ideas

34 Above L: *Movable sale and theme tables.* Kepler's Books & Magazines, Menlo Park, Calif.
33 Above R: *A quilt print table cloth* used to attract attention and set the theme for this table display. Davis Kidd Bookstore, Memphis, Tenn.
35 Right: *Low, open base sale table* and hospitality basket display.
36 Below: *Sale book table.* Sign promises 75 percent off remainders. Both: Airport Shop, Detroit, Mich.

window, in the store, on floor stands, or on table top displays.

Foam core and gator boards can be recycled and covered with felt, fabric, decorative wrapping paper, contact paper, brown Kraft, and even news paper pages ▲44. Fringe, trimmings, and other ornamentation can add flavor and interest to these panels. Trimmings should be used with taste and discretion. Small holes can be cut or drilled through the boards to mount all sorts of theme and seasonal ornaments such as pine cones, Christmas ornaments, or shells. Rope lights can be poked through the openings to create borders and patterns of twinkling lights ▲32.

Foam core and gator board are both available from stationers, art stores, and display houses. Sizes range from 24" x 30" to 48" x 96" and thicknesses from 3/16" to 3/4". When larger sizes are needed, join two pieces of the

same material together with a reinforcing strip of wood. They may also be pasted onto larger sheets of corrugated board. Several thicknesses of boards can be bonded together with spray adhesive to make a panel of any thickness, and foam core and gator boards are easy to cut and shaped with a sharp razor knife.

Lattice Panels and Screens

Remember the white lattice work in the film *Mary Poppins* and the race track scene at Ascot in *My Fair Lady*? Scenic and display designers have for years relied on lattice work to create fanciful, romantic backgrounds. Why not join them? Lattice panels are used in display work for the same reasons they are used in film and theatre set decorations. Lattice panels add texture and quality perceptions to the setting.

Lattice panels are thin strips of wood manufactured and assembled into convenient one-piece, 24" x 96" to 48" x 96" panels. It is possible to spray paint lattice panels any color. You can quickly change the mood by simply painting the lattice a color to compliment the theme of your display.

For a change of character you can create an "Old Banana Republic" look by staining the wood lattices to blend with the mood of your display and surrounding natural wood store fixtures, furniture, or flooring. Stunning combinations of striking colors can be generated by adding colored papers or fabrics, sections of mirror, and shiny vinyl to the back of the lattice. Lighting lattice panels from the back creates

37 Right: *Puzzle mobile* is attention-grabbing device above business book display. Borders Books & Music, Phoenix, Ariz.
38 Below: *Pattern table cloth* with Afro-American colors and pattern motif to call attention to theme table display. B&N, New York, N.Y.

39 Right: *Hospitality baskets and theme table cloth* in children's book department. Borders Books & Music, Columbus, Ohio.

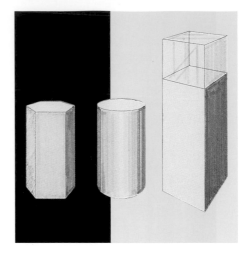

40 Left: ***Two-level display cubes*** *(risers) used to organize upscale display of jewelry.* 41 Right: ***Pedestals*** *are available in different sizes, shapes, and heights. Museum-type security tops are also available.*

striking shadow patterns that add dimension to the background. Adding and lighting sheets of colored gelatin to the back of the lattice produces a remarkable stained glass effect. Cross lighting creates shadows and adds interest. Standard grid wall display system accessories can be modified and adapted to hang onto lattice panels. This feature makes it possible and practical to hang merchandise, displays, signs, ornaments, and wreaths on the lattice. Let your imagination run wild with the design and visual merchandising opportunities lattices and other movable backings offer you.

Lattice panels are moderately priced and relatively easy to install. They are sometimes connected to a ceiling grid with sky hooks ▲32. Tie the panel to the display floor with brads tied into filament fish line to keep the lattice panels from swaying. Lattice panels can also be mounted directly to flush walls and column surfaces. Lattice panels can also be put into door, window, and large picture frames, and they can be mounted on legs and braces to use as floor display backings ▲160.

Folding Screens

Folding screens can be relied on as a window divider or as a backing ▲32. Folding screens are available in modern and traditional design styles. Low, 30" to 40" high screens can be successfully integrated into open-back window displays. High 72" to 96" screens work well in closed-back windows because they are usually finished on two sides.

Open frame, folding screens are also commercially available. Use them to fill in with cloth, stained glass, mirror, or your own art panels.

Display Cubes, Pedestals, and Chairs

Display cubes, also known as stacker boxes, are the extraordinary versatile work horses of the display business. Display cubes (stacker boxes) can be several empty cartons stacked in a pattern, and wrapped with colorful paper or fabric ▲43, 159, wood boxes painted or stained, or plastic crates or boxes made of particle board and stained a funky aniline color with dye. As the

name implies, stacker boxes are placed on the floor and stacked one on the other at the end of or on table tops ▲158. Cubes are versatile. They are sometimes wood crates faced in and sometimes out with products arranged both in and on top of the box. Sturdy cubes are just as useful on the end of gondolas ▲140a. There they serve as the base for quantities of a single title. Cubes are wonderful places to stack games and boxed merchandise ▲60.

Cubes 8" to 10" high are useful on table tops because that is the height of most trade and reference books. The cubes can be stacked one on the other to create a higher level. For large table presentations, cubes can be arranged one tier above the other to create a step pyramid effect and act as a base for a promotion sign.

Small cubes for use in showcases are made in clear acrylic, painted, stained, and laminate finishes from 3" to 8" squares and may be custom-ordered in any height or finish needed ▲40. Display cubes are available in square, triangular, hexagonal, semicircular, and circular shapes. Heights

42 Above: **Chanukah theme** *display is set with table cloths, menorah, and an orderly arrangement of books.*

44 Below: **Father's Day.** *A great sign backed with foam core and paper bag props combine on this tabletop and riser for a Father's (Dad's) Day promotion. Bollingers Books, Oklahoma City, Okla.*

43 Above: **Boxes covered with gift wrappings for risers.** *Ornaments suspended with ribbons create a festive Christmas gift theme.* Shakespear & Co., New York, N.Y.

45 Left: *Bamboo blinds can provide inexpensive window backing.* 46 Center: *Venetian blinds can be spray painted to coordinate with a particular theme and control natural light.* 47 Right: *Colored and pattern design roller shades can provide a foil for theme merchandise presentation.*

can vary from 3" to 24," at which point display cubes cross become pedestals ▲60, 65. Pedestals are vertical stands made of plastic, composition stone, cardboard tubes, wood, and wood products. Pedestals are used to elevate merchandise for effective visual presentation.

The styles of pedestals vary from contemporary shafts to classical Greek columns and are available from 6" to 6' high. Large 24" to 30" wide Corinthian column capitols painted interesting colors make wonderful table bases ▲85. Columns may be colored with spray paint or covered with wallpaper to create a beautiful marble effect in any color. A Corinthian column painted white is a marvelous base for travel books to the Greek Islands. Use a pink column with a cerulian blue base for books on Hawaii. The same column painted metallic gold makes a stunning base for Christmas gift books. Black columns make an elegant pedestal base for design and decorating titles.

Pedestals are reasonably priced and available from many display supply houses. Step stairs and stools are useful in raising key selections, and other props, or giving depth to window trims ▲48.

The Display Calendar

Successful DVM comes from piecing together the decisions of the owner, manager, merchandisers and advertising and promotion staff into a working plan. Good window display and store-wide visual merchandise presentation is the coming together of a one-of-a-kind merchandise event.

The display calendar is the planning document that details schedules and responsibility to coordinate the installation of the display. No matter how abstract the nature of it's contents, the plan provides a working baseline.

Blocked out a year in advance, the best DVM calendars incorporate the notes and ideas for future DVM plans. The plan describes what is to happen in the future as things now stand. By definition the DVM plan is always a flexible document subject to instant change. The display calendar can be used to help keep displays and merchandise moving smoothly in and out of the display windows; on and off sale tables, end-caps, and promotional pieces. As seen in table 3, lead time is essential for listing predetermined slots that schedule in-store and annual events. These entered into the schedule provide a reminder in one place and help keep the store looking new, fresh, and exciting. The DVM schedule anticipates the arrival of new books and merchandise that flow through the store all year long. The American Booksellers (ABA) and other trade groups prepare and distribute annual merchandising calendars to their members. These are good marketing tools and a benefit of membership in the ABA. They can help you. Use them to establish your DVM schedule.

When to Change Window Displays

Displays in the windows of stores in fashionable areas such as upper Fifth Avenue, along Chicago's "miracle mile," and the high streets of London are usually set every two weeks. The stores in more characteristic locations are changed once every month. A wild card – a new blockbuster book title – arrives out of sequence, or a significant event develops in the community, the country, or the world takes place, and the decision is made for a quick change of the display to "tie into" the event. When this happens, smile, shrug your shoulders, and get on with it. Be flexible. Respond to the need with a quick window and interior display change. Take advantage of what may turn out to be a window of opportunity. Give it your best shot.

Preparing to Display Merchandise

The design of the show window display begins by determining the display technique to use. Determine how you will actually present the products you have selected. Picture in your mind the most appealing and practical approach available. For example; will you use pedestals, easels, and roll down shades to convey your merchandising offer?

Next, envision how you will arrange and highlight the products to be displayed. Visualize how you will position each item in the display. Do this in your mind or on a sketch pad. At this stage of the design development you may sense the need for a prop or spot of color to heighten the show-stopping quality of your presentation.

The third step is to select the background you feel will best work with the color scheme and type of lighting to produce the mood and theme you have decided upon. Next, choose the props ◆74. The choice of the props should go hand-in-hand with the mood and theme of the window and fill any gaps or holes in the presentation. The props need not be placed according to any rules, but they should not divert attention from the merchandise. The goal is to create an appealing arrangement.

Here's the tough part. The final step is to make a rough sketch of the display that you are proposing. Even a rough sketch will help you when you begin to assemble the display. A sketch will also allow your management to see what you

---

Table 3: Lead Time for Preparing Integrated Display and Visual Merchandising Plans

The preparation of the best integrated display and visual merchandising plans begins ninety days in advance of the launch date.

Theme/Season	Plan Month	Promotion Month
Fall	September October November	December January February
Winter	December January February	March April May
Spring	March April May	June July August
Summer	June July August	September October November

Illusion in Show Window Display

Garland winding up to top of the tree – that isn't!

48 Above L: *The illusion of a Christmas tree is masterfully created in theme setting. The triangular construction begins by raising the focal point of the display up onto chair seats. Gracefully laced garlands of hemlock brass ribbon and ornaments wind up the back of the window to the top of the window fixture and then up onto heavy, bark covered branches at the top.* 49 Above R: **Detail photo** *is found at the right.* Scribner, New York, N.Y.

Fabric covered show window floor with glitter

Wrapped presents

Fabric covered board across chair seats

Show window backing

Face up display on easels

Open book

THE MASTER JEWELERS

Teddy bear

Three opera chairs spray painted gold

Hemlock garland rope with pine cones

Burnished gold ribbon

Three sample books each stepped back

Related titles

Table 4: List of Typical Display Handtools

1. GUIDING TOOLS
   a. straight edge
   b. square
   c. 12" level
   d. plumb bob
2. MARKING TOOLS
   a. chalk line
   b. pencil
   c. scratch awl
   d. scriber
   e. compass and divider
3. MEASURING TOOLS
   a. rule
   b. tape

4. HOLDING TOOLS
   a. pliers
   b. clamps
   c. vises
5. CUTTING TOOLS
   a. saws
   b. files
   c. rasps
   d. chisels
   e. knives
   f. wire cutters
   g. shears
   h. scissors
6. SCRAPING TOOLS
   a. scrapers
   b. sand paper

7. BORING TOOLS
   a. battery-powered hand drill
   b. bits
   c. drills
   d. countersinks
8. LEVELING TOOLS
   a. bubble level
   b. line level
9. FASTENING TOOLS
   a. hammers
   b. screw drivers
   c. wrenches
   d. battery-powered screw driver

---

are planning. They may have suggestions. Pay attention to them. It will be much easier to deal with adjustments in a sketch of a display arrangement than to rearrange the complete window display after the window trim is completed.

At this juncture begin by collecting the books and merchandise to be featured in the window design. Ask yourself:

- Is the mood I am trying to capture compatible with the merchandise I plan to display?
- Does the item fit with the color scheme and theme I have chosen?
- Are all the pieces of a similar texture and style and age appeal, or does it matter?
- Will I use a multi-title, multi-merchandise presentation of a single category or focus on a single title merchandise presentation?
- Are the textures selected for window backing compatible with the merchandise and the theme?

- Will the amount of merchandise selected work with the display space available?
- Is the merchandise selected susceptible to damage from temperature extremes–will it freeze, fade, or melt in the show window?

As you gather merchandise for the display, stack it neatly in a tote box, on a cart, or hang it from a cart riser. When possible, move your merchandise, tools, and props on a cart to the area where the display is to be arranged.

Advance Preparation

Spend as much time as possible preparing window and interior signs in advance, selecting and arranging table cloths and flowers, gathering information, promotional posters, and other media. This preparation will ease some of the pressure when the time comes to put in the displays. It's best to start your work in the display windows early in the

morning, an hour before the store opens. This will allow time to prepare the display area, sometimes a noisy, messy operation, before customers arrive. There is another practical reason for starting early. Did anyone ever tell you that show windows get hot in the summer or that you can freeze in winter? Depending on the orientation of the store front, starting early may permit you to set up most of the window before the sun rises too high and you begin to bake in the afternoon heat.

Show Time

At long last you are ready to start the installation of the show window design. The following steps are common to most window displays:

- If a change of wall or floor covering is required, change it first.
- Move any props you have selected into the display.
- Assemble and position your

---

means of display: pedestals, suspended panels, easels.

- Place your merchandise on or around them.
- Adjust the lights to illuminate the areas you want to highlight.
- Finally, add the window signs to the setting.

Display Tools

A few important tools are required for the preparation and installation of display work. At a minimum you will need a pair of pliers, a tack and claw hammer, scissors, a loaded staple (tacking) gun, a utility knife, and a small stepladder.

We suggest you buy two tool boxes with locks. Use the first tool box for your hand tools. Tools tend to disappear if they are not secured. If you chose to buy a combination lock, buy one with a changeable combination. If the need develops, change the combination, providing the new combination only to those you know to be trustworthy. Consider buying a can of fluorescent spray paint to mark a band on your hand tools. The color band will make it easier to spot your tools in the midst of setting up a display and could remove any question of ownership. Use the second tool

box for the adhesives, threads, tapes, and miscellaneous accessories needed for DVM. It will save you time and frustration if your display materials are consolidated in one place. Each time you change the show window you will find a dustpan and brush helpful to clean the display area. If the floor is carpeted, a hand-held Dust Buster vacuum may be just the tool you need.

Tools are needed for guiding, marking, measuring, holding, cutting, scraping, boring, leveling, and fastening. Table 4 will give you an idea of the kinds of display hand tools needed to do the job.

As we move from this broad discussion of the mechanics of organizing and installing a show window design, the next step is to determine if the display you have in mind requires a special appeal or if the display must be set in a particular mood.

It is crucial that displays be installed when customer interest is developing.

The display should continue until interest has diminished.

★ ★ ★ ★ ★

There's lots, lots more to this story, as we shall see in chapter 3 following.

DVM Design

3

To plan and carry out show window design with traffic-stopping appeal, a retailer need not have extensive training or a large display budget, but must have a clear understanding of the image of the store and the clientele it serves. This may not be as easy as it sounds.

This chapter deals with insight into blending the essential elements of color, light, balance, focus, and harmony to develop the customized mood and emotional appeal in DVM designs. These combined elements form an image which relates to every aspect of the DVM project. Images are sometimes dismissed as impermanent, intangible, and valueless. The reality is that the impact of an image is so potent it is often the store's most valuable asset.

Image by Choice

Because image is so important, the problem is making conscious decisions about image rather than letting them be made by default. How a store's image is perceived by the customer–the visual expressions of its identity–will in large measure determine how the company and its products and services are valued by its customers.

The public sees logos, unique color schemes, and other visual elements of bookstores every day. Although surveys show that we think people don't pay much attention to them, they do. Sometimes a logo or color scheme takes on a vitality of its own and goes beyond its function as a symbol appearing on a newsletter or at the bottom of an advertisement. It can become the body and soul of a store.

Images are important. Companies are continually sending out visual and verbal messages to change or to strengthen their image in the marketplace. Eighty-five percent of what we learn is perceived through our eyes. The visual element of any image, therefore, is extremely important. The design elements of identity are the things that last. Long after the effect of opinions expressed in words have dissipated, the visual elements remain. DVM graphic design systems can represent the single most significant capital expenditure associated with the implementation of a new store identity.

Permanent Image-Building Elements

DVM design programs contain both permanent and changeable components. The permanent ones are considered the traditional mainstays of a business identity. Catalogues, store bags, advertising, book marks, menus, stationary, buildings, motor vehicle policy, and control signage are the principal items.

50 Left: *Fresh flowers and live plants* add a new concept that feels remarkably familiar, comfortable, and *welcome*. Bollingers Books, Oklahoma City, Okla.

51 Right: *Consistent day and night image* presented by design of store entrance. BOOKS-A-MILLION, Daytona Beach, Fla.

52 Below: *Unique name*, simple letter style sign, and bright awning highlight front and entrance image of Noodle Kidoodle, Paramus, N.J.

53 Bottom: *The distinctive curvature* of the front gives a unique identity to MEDIA PLAY, Columbus, Ohio.

These graphic items lend themselves to tight control for consistency. Combined, they produce the maximum impact.

Changeable Image-Building Elements

In-store sales promotional materials and displays change from month to month. They must be flexible and easily modified at the drop of a hat. They must respond to changing market conditions and successfully promote and grow the image of the store. In developing an image, stores can and should consider the following:

1. *Identify who you are.* A retail bookstore must have a clear statement of identity from which to build. This statement of identity takes into account the store's history and unique strengths. Owners, ask yourself, "Where has this company been? What worked best for it as it was growing? Is it still working?" If you don't know who you are, how can the customer ever know?

2. *Identify what you do.* There must be a clear statement of purpose. What is your business? What are its priorities? Where is the store heading? What are its objectives? Ask yourself, "How do I want to be perceived?" Establish a clear and concise statement of purpose.

3. *Align the store with your stated identity.* Adopt practices that will communicate your image. Customer perceptions of the store must be the same as the image the store wants to project.

Valentine's Day

Begin with a sweetheart pink and white end-cap poster. Add scalloped paper shelf edging, and sign listing tie-in titles. Market gift-wrapped sidelines and gift certificates here.

Saint Patrick's Day

Gather up a collection of good titles and try your luck with a set of four-leaf clover posters to get your share of the customers' attention on St. Patrick's Day.

Gardening Theme

Mount a painted trellis border on a foamcore backing. Add drawings of planting tools, plants, flowers, and seeds onto the backing. Make painted trellis panels and attach them to the ends of table risers and end panels.

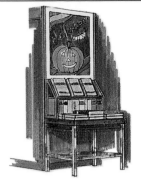

Halloween

Try gold lettering on a grey background to highlight a big, friendly, orange pumpkin to sprinkle a contemporary color flavor into your end-cap display.

TEN IDEAS TO HELP YOU GET STARTED WITH END-CAP MERCHANDISING

Easter - Kids

Make (or buy) a set of posters and use them on end-caps, sides of windows, and columns to announce your Easter promotion. Pink, lavender, plush animals, and Easter eggs add to the visual excitement. Use a chicken fat yellow shelf ledge paper in highlight areas.

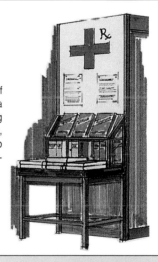

Health - Well-Being

Red Cross symbols cut out of foamcore and mounted on a white foamcore board. Hang these above a display of health, medical, and titles related to well-being. This idea is powerful enough to affect sales.

Mother's Day

Choose a pattern of wall paper that reflects your store. Mount it, or them, to cover a full height gator board panel. Overlay the panel with "Mother's Day" signs. Display special titles and gift certificates.

Flag Day, Memorial Day, and Independence Day

Use painted and miniature flags fastened to a gator board backing. Feature titles at this location. Consider attaching striped fabric to sides and columns with double face tape.

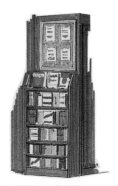

Nonfiction Reviews

Add a tack board to your end-cap and post book reviews, forthcoming, and new release information.

Entertainment - Home Furnishings - Collections

Make a full height foamcore end-cap backing panel. Wrap it with distinctive fabric, change the fabric every ninety days to "Hail the coming season." This will help build customers awareness of the display.

Designing for Mood and Appeal

The underlying notion of a show window design is the mix of its emotional appeal, its balance, focus, harmony of arrangement, and the color and lighting used in its composition. Whenever they are brought together, the combination of these elements must reflect the image of the store.

The presentation of information in the design and layout of the display often takes on a character all it's own. Here is where the mood and emotional appeal of the design relate to the image of the store. For example, imagine a window display with a white background with white display cubes featuring beautifully bound and illustrated books. Now, visualize these books supported by acrylic easels and made more distinctive by a pinpoint spotlight focused on the books. Picture the display supported by distinctive window sign cards to provide additional information to the customer. The sum of all the points in this display conveys the image of a quality bookstore.

The distinctiveness of the presentation, it's simplicity and plainness combine to create a unique feeling that communicates more than subtle information. It transmits the image of quality and completeness in the display.

When window displays present a striking design, customers respond immediately to it. This is true even from a distance before the customer actually recognizes the merchandise. The customer's opinion of the display is based solely on the mood or

appeal it presents. If the viewer has a good impression and the display has aroused a "rush of emotions," if the level of customer inquisitiveness is raised, then the mood of the display is a smashing success. This is the emotional appeal of the display.

Emotional Appeal

Remembering that the goal is to attract interest and amuse or stimulate the mind, first consider the title, cover, and subject matter of the book you plan to feature, and how the color, quality, and props you have in mind relate to the subject.

Does the title itself suggest a particular emotion? Is the emotion one of love, hate, war or peace? Does the subject focus on nostalgia, fashion, or taste? Does the subject lend itself to a particular season or some business phenomena?

Before deciding on a particular prop ask yourself, "to whom am I appealing?" Is the target market an upscale clientele with an old world/tres chic feel? Does the design, color, and mood give the store an exclusive image? Is that image right for our market or is it uninviting to the middle market, the one we reach?

Is the emotional appeal to the up market also inviting and comfortable to the middle market? Is it also especially appealing to the market of women shoppers in your locality or is your appeal really that of a classic American bookstore with a tasteful collection of gift merchandise? Will the appeal of the display have the power to attract, create interest, amuse or stimulate the mind and emotions of your customers? These are good questions. To help

get some answers, consider the following:

Creating the Mood

The emotion you want to project will help you decide the type of mood to design ▲1. For example, to appeal to your customers' interest in travel, your window design could project a sense of time, space, adventure, information, motion, and the facts about getting there. The display could also talk about what to do when you arrive, and how to communicate with local residents. Could the appeal be reinforced with language dictionaries and electronic language translators?

It is important to decide how broadly the mood will pervade your design. Will the travel window include travel posters, maps and globes, luggage and travel accessories? Will it be declared boldly, with every piece in the presentation dedicated to one idea, so the customer will not miss the point? Will merchandise on display be priced? Let's look at another example.

Consider the mood you would choose for a theme to be built entirely around back-to-school books and teacher's aids. Will you have the customary apple for the teacher, coloring books, crayons, paint sets, and other learning tools? Will the mood be bright and cheerful? Will it project a sense of anticipation and fun that parents, grandparents, and kids enjoy? Of course it should.

Creating Themes

Any mood that you may want to create can be supported with several possible themes, but understand that not everyone view-

Die cut, store-wide theme poster dangler

Oversize papier-mâché apples and pears with branch props

Information sign to help locate these titles inside the store

Vertical lighting track

Fifth row displayed on riser shelves with display cubes to gain an additional display level

Fourth row on white shelf

Third row of face-forward titles

Second row face forward on cubes

First row uses vertical front and back, spine out arrangement with flat books which creates an interesting visual break

55 Above: *Anatomy of an asymmetrical show window display.* This would be suitable for a small store. DILLON'S, London, U.K.

ing a merchandise presentation will sense exactly the same thing.

The display of home entertainment titles surrounded by colored balloons, shimmering danglers, and ribbons may seem natural, fun and fanciful to one person, but it may look like a background for a sit-com or "Saturday Night Live" to another.

Serious booksellers usually serving the academic community prefer to keep their window presentations very simple and direct. They often rely on a no-nonsense approach that combines certain classifications of books with unique customer appeal in windowed areas. They may focus on the titles of a single publisher, on an author, or on new quality bound editions, fictions, and literature ▲59. These types of informative displays are simple to maintain, yet can

project an image of genuine seriousness. These simple displays can also be integrated with a more lively presentation. For example, they can be trimmed with garlands and rope lights to create a festive Christmas season theme.

Consider all of the implications of your design to make sure its theme creates the appeal you are trying to initiate and compliments the image of the store.

Choosing the Right Theme

Once you decide on a theme to develop, make sure it is not too focused and limited. Make a positive choice and stick with it through the design process and installation of the design.

Look around you. Check your competition and the stores you respect. Make a scrap book of

ideas and things to remember. Check the ABA Merchandising Calendar for timely ideas. Check with your publisher's representatives about upcoming titles, title promotions using character costumes, and available dealer aides. Save the designs you develop so that they may be referred to and improved on next year. You will be surprised at how much information is out there to challenge your thinking and waiting to be used.

Do not confuse the customer with too many ideas. Resist any themes not consistent with your store image. You will only lose if you try to take sides in a debated issue. You could alienate a market segment that is important to your business.

After you decide on a particular theme, try experimenting with the color, light, display set pieces,

Vertical lighting

Open view into the store

Beautiful cloud theme hanging backdrop

Summer theme logo used repeatedly in window and throughout store

Four levels of display

Gold leaf logo applied to glass

56 Above: *Summer reading theme* in a closed-back asymmetrical theme window. DILLON'S, London, U.K.

Boomer men are rarely interested in displays with emotional appeal.

Expensive, trendy color settings appeal and attract boomer women.

Design show windows with themes that can be transferred to the interior of the store.

The aggregate of merchandise, information signs, backing, and lighting form the character of a display design.

Color, light, and textures that subtly relate to the subject of a title adds to the completeness of the presentation. They reinforce the mood and emotional appeal of the display design.

Before you start, know what merchandise you will be working with.

Select moods and themes that are simple and work well together.

Keep an eye on what your competition is doing.

Make and maintain a log of display ideas for future reference.

and props to use. Good color and great lighting help unify the theme presentation. Together they suggest "a right reason" for the titles displayed together ▲56. Take care that the mood you choose is sensible and in keeping with the image of your store, but keep it light. Recognize who your customers are. Apply Golden Rule Number 2: Do not under or overestimate the intelligence of your boss–the customer.

No Mood At All

Many store owners successfully rely on the balance, focus, and harmony of titles displayed to touch a sympathetic chord, and create the image they wish to convey without appearing dull or languid.

If your store windows are not located to attract the attention of regular customers and people passing by, you may decide that a neutral mood–no mood at all– is the best approach for your window presentation. The best approach for you may be to concentrate on exhibiting basic store information, such as the monthly calendar of events (one of our favorite ideas), store hours, location of the store within a building, index of services, and telephone and fax numbers. Neutral displays may also include a lighted store map and list of the book category offered by the store.

Avoid looking insignificant, amateurish, or inconsequential at all costs. Take care that the window backings, stands, pedestals, easels, and other display devices used in the neutral mood presentation create a favorable, professional impression in keeping with your business.

Easel-backed books | Draped window floor | Draped cubes and risers

Vertical books on flat books | Draped cube | Draped platform risers

57 Top: *Asymmetrical multi-title display*. Scribner, New York, N.Y.
58 Above: *Symmetrical display - multi-title display*. Scribner, New York, N.Y.
59 Below: *Monthly Spotlight - asymmetric display features a multi-title presentation of one author's work*. Harvard Bookstore, Cambridge, Mass.

3-D Effect

Use a 3-D effect to create a direct and forceful visual merchandise presentation at the front of the store. Each level of the presentation can be used to focus attention on a single item or group of items.

Tallest gondola – 84-96"

High gondola – 54-60"

Medium gondola – 54-60"

Low table – 28-32"

60 Left: ***Arranging tabletop display*** *heights from low to high suggests visual movement that leads the eye from display to display. The success of storefront merchandising depends on the composition of the presentation.* Learningsmith, Palo Alto, Calif.

61 Below: ***High ceiling and corner space*** *is open, bright, and divided by high, center-floor gondolas, a live tree, and comfortable furniture where "cowboys" can browse through selections from philosophy to western civilization.* BookPeople Bookstore & Café, Austin, Tex.

Timing Mood Displays and Themes

The natural calendar of retail promotions is the time when all other retail outlets combine to promote a certain national or regional promotional event. Key promotional events occur on Valentine's Day, Mother's Day, Father's Day, the Fourth of July, Back-to-School, Halloween, Veteran's Day, Election Day, Thanksgiving, Hanukkah, and Christmas. In these instances, retailers in general combine to create the "mood" of the event and raise its emotional appeal. Stores with the right level of appeal tie into these community events. These are the times to make sure the store is "especially attractive and pleasing, and an interesting place to be." Be competitive. You will enjoy your success more.

Symmetrical Balance

Symmetrical balance has an easy flow. It is easy to understand and generally the best place to start. To use the principal of symmetrical balance in your design, begin by positioning the main point of interest. This will be the key item that you intend to feature in the display. Next, position all the shapes and the methods of presentation to lead the eye up invisible "flight" lines to the main point of interest, thus forming an invisible triangle.

Books and sidelines do not have to be lined up like cork bobs on a fish line, but their forms and colors should present a pleasing flow right up the flight lines to loosely resemble the form of the invisible triangle. If your design were cut down through the middle, each half would be a

62 Above: ***Changing the color of the floor covering*** *creates separation between titles and helps customer selection.* B&D, Bad Hammon, Ger.
63 Below: ***Beach/vacation theme*** *in closed-back, asymmetrical theme window.* B&N, New York, N.Y.

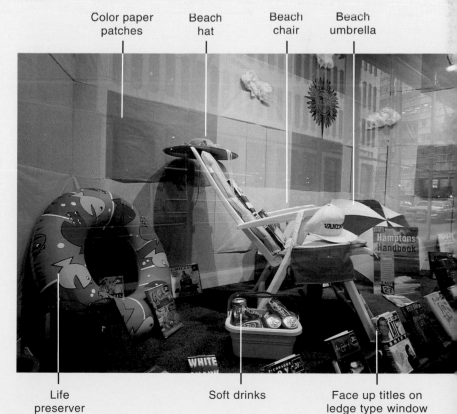

Color paper patches — Beach hat — Beach chair — Beach umbrella

Life preserver — Soft drinks — Face up titles on ledge type window platform

Bunting

64 Right: *Anatomy of the symmetric title page window.* Scribner, New York, N.Y.
65 Below: *Detail of bunting draped over display steps.* Scribner, New York, N.Y.

Applied vinyl gold leaf lettering on glass

Books on easels
Oversized title
Center pedestal
Bunting drapery folded over floor, plus four-row high step units or folding bleacher seats

reflection of the other half. This type of display is a classical example of symmetrical balance ▲25.

The underlying principal of symmetrical balance is to match, or balance, the books and merchandise waiting to be displayed with display pedestals and cubes, window signs, color, and texture so the customers visual interest will be guided up each side of the invisible triangle. This visual flow will lead the viewer to the focal point, or as they say in the movies, to the "pay-off spot," the place where the most important item in the display is located.

Asymmetrical Balance ▲31

The second approach employs asymmetrical or informal balance. Asymmetrical balance is a less formal arrangement. Although it is more complicated to envision and implement, asymmetrical balance is often a more interesting approach to window display. In concept, the two sides of the display are similar although not exact reflections of each other. However, they are said to be of equal weight. Equal weight means there is a visual balance in

the two sides of the display. The asymmetrical balance of window designs is based upon use of negative and positive space.

Start by positioning large, eye catching, merchandise and props along one of the flight lines, just as we did in achieving symmetrical balance. This is the positive space. This will be the spot where the element in the display that first catches the viewer's attention is located. Now, either locate low props up the other flight line or leave the space empty. This is the negative space. We call it negative space because it does not vie for attention. The negative space will, however, visually route the viewer's eye back to the positive space.

Consequently, viewers interest will first be attracted to the large object (the positive space). Depending upon your design, viewers attention will flow up the flight lines to the focal point and down again to low lying objects or empty space.

Needless to say, the selection of backgrounds against which these designs play is important. When your design is conceptualized, make sure there is a continuous visual flow from one element to the next, keeping in mind that the flight line from the negative space is invisible. For this reason, it is best not to locate any books or merchandise in this negative space.

Interior Display

The principals for achieving balance in window design also apply to achieving visual balance in the interior displays. Unlike closed–back show windows, interior display spaces are not rigidly bound on four sides. Customers generally view interior displays from several perspectives.

Large interior display statements can start at the floor or begin on a platform at the front of the store. They can be found on a table top at an aisle intersection or in "found" space at the end of a main customer traffic aisle. These are known as strike zones. Strike zones are the important locations where well-coordinated DVM displays can be a particular product. They allow you to "strike while the iron is hot, hit the mark, and make your point."

Since you will not have as much visual control over the interior space as you would with a show window, you might find it practical to begin with symmetrical designs for in-house displays.

Start by arranging interior table tops, small end-caps, ledge, showcase, and shelf displays using the principle of invisible triangles.

Displays with invisible triangular arrangements can appear storewide in dozens of locations. At peak periods they should be frequently rearranged in the span of a single day to keep the product looking fresh and not picked over "as stock is sold down."

The important visual expressions of a store's identity will in large measure determine how the store, its products, and its services are valued by its customers and audiences.

Do not confuse the customer with too many ideas.

At all cost, avoid looking insignificant, amateurish, or inconsequential.

Of all forms, the triangle is the most adaptable to visual merchandising.

Symmetrical balance has an easy visual flow and is easy to understand.

Asymmetrical balance is less formal but can be a more interesting approach to design.

Interior displays are generally viewed from several perspectives.

★ ★ ★ ★ ★

Next let's look at the importance of creating consistent visual messages.

SALE BOOKS

Creating a Consistent Visual Message with Balance, Focus, Harmony, Lighting, and Color

4

The visual part of DVM pertains to the external and internal look and feel of the display composition. When the grouping, arrangement of merchandise, the tone, atmosphere, and visual character of the retail store are unified by the consistent application of these principles, a store image is formed. Its fair to say that the impact can be substantial. Let us look at each of these important segments of the DVM concept.

Balance, Focus, and Harmony

Balance, focus, and harmony are the three essentials of display composition. Balance describes a pleasing grouping that is neither top-heavy nor lopsided. Focus is the eye-catching, visual flow of the display. Visual focus is achieved through the use of harmonizing or contrasting colors, lighting, changes of texture, or through the use of an unusual accessory or prop in the display setting.

Harmony is the pleasing compliment of books and merchandise within the window display environment and in-store merchandising. Contrast and proportion are also important to the display equation.

Why Balance?

A display should be well balanced, if for no other reason than it makes customers feel more comfortable. Well-balanced displays are more easily compared and understood by the viewer.

The theme for displays found in the windows of most independent bookstores focuses on books and more books, with only an occasional regard to balance, focus, or harmony. If some energy, a few cubes and pedestals to break up the monotony, some information signs to inform, display arrows to focus attention, and color blocks are added to the display, a better display will be achieved and more products will be sold.

When the display design elements of balance, focus, and harmony interact properly with one another, they take on a dynamic character and "Wow!" appeal of their own.

Why Focus?

When visual elements are combined in a balanced arrangement, the customer's visual attention is focused on either a single idea or on a number of items. Focus deals with how the eye moves to recognize all parts of the display statement. Customers naturally scan visual information in the same

66 Left: *Skylight floods sunlight* over this interior garden room. Flexible, black floor cases are moved to make room for *author presentations and discussions.* Bookshop, Santa Cruz, Calif.

order in which they read a book. In most cultures this means from left to right, from top to bottom, and from front to back. It is important to keep this visual hierarchy in mind because the focus of a display can be targeted onto the single item by (a) moving the item forward from back to front; (b) by moving it to the left side; (c) by elevating it from the bottom to the top; (d) highlighting it with a graphic device such as an arrow or a four leaf clover; (e) highlighting it with color; or (f) illuminating it with a pool of light.

Focus customers attention on the merchandise and graphics in displays by taking advantage of these "attention grabbing" principles.

Customers who regularly read Asian languages tend to look from right to left because their eyes have been trained to look immediately at the top right of a printed page.

Why Harmony?

Harmony is the pleasing grouping of books and merchandise, props, and signs.

While visual harmony emphasizes similarities, visual contrast emphasizes pleasing visual differences. These differences might be shown by contrasting soft pastel colors with the starkness of primary colors or by contrasting the roundness of spheres and globes with the sharp edges of triangles and cubes. Visual contrast can also be seen by comparing thick and thin, light and heavy rope, or between bright and dim light when used in a single composition.

Use contrast to intensify (or hold back) both the properties

67 Above: *Artwork hung from ceiling in window. Symmetrical arrangement permits different categories to be featured on individual display tables.* Carolus Buchundkunst, Frankfurt, Ger.
68 Above R: *Posters and promotional material announcing a new title and author's scheduled signing.* Carolus Buchundkunst, Frankfurt, Ger.
69 Right: *Face-up display of CD's, related book titles, and a poster hung from the ceiling in an open-back window.* Frankfurt, Ger.
70 Below: *Foam core-backed poster announcing a storewide sale of books and music.* Frankfurt, Ger.

71 Above L: **Low T-walls** *form alcoves to personalize title sections, provide a place for reading, and personal selection.* Frankfurt, Ger.

72 Above R: *A* **barber chair** *with a view of the parking lot below adds a bit of humor to a serious bookstore.* BookPeople Bookstore & Coffeehouse, Austin, Tex.

73: Right: **Travel theme presentation** *in an open-back asymmetrical window display arrangement.* Phileas Fogg's Books & More, Palo Alto, Calif.

(light or dark) and position (size and thickness) of each element employed in the window design. Harmonious differences in color, texture, and props will also heighten viewers interest and attract attention to a particular display.

Lighting

Bright lighting is appropriate in all selling environments.

74 Above: **Red neon exterior lighting** *that surrounds the top row of show windows across the front which faces Broadway and vividly establishes the size of and calls attention to* Tower Records, New York, N.Y.

75 Center L: **Softer exterior neon** *colors used in* Tower Records, Annapolis, Md.

76 Center R: **Green exterior neon** *surrounds show window in* Paramus, N.J.

77 Bottom: **High-gloss show window** *is covered with etched glass decal and backlighted to highlight small, expensive items.* San Francisco International, Calif.

Straight, continuous rows of bright exposed lamps in display windows and interiors create a deep, discount bargain-book look ▲155, 186. Interesting arrangements of overlapping and staggered rows of bright fluorescent lighting can also be used to create fresh and pleasant moods. High levels of lighting contribute to the sales atmosphere for children's fiction and literature ▲79.

What once took high wattage track fixtures to accomplish can now be done with concealed compact fluorescent lamps. In addition, feature displays can be made to "pop" with excitement by using the new halogen IR lamps. Additionally, these systems consume from 30 to 50 percent less energy than previous lighting systems and dramatically change the appeal of store displays.

Dim overall lighting with highlighted areas can be used to create dramatic moods. Dimmed lighting can also be a helpful technique to create a mysterious and even sinister type settings appropriate to the marketing of mystery, ghost, horror, classics, and other literary classifications.

Compared to colder versions of daylight or warm white, new fluorescent and octron lamps produce a desirable quality of light suitable for the marketing of technical and reference books ▲80. Compact fluorescent "wall washer" lamp fixtures with only 24-inch long bulbs that are recessed into the ceiling or mounted on lighting tracks have emerged as one of the best new ways to light walls and wall cases straight up from the floor to the ceiling in bookstores. In most retail store situations compact, high-output 25-watt fluorescent lamps are now mixed with incandescent

78 Above: *Well designed show window* illuminated on three sides. London, U.K.

lamps to reduce energy consumption and the excess heat generated by normal incandescent lamps.

The mix of strategically placed low-voltage incandescent and compact high-intensity lamps can also produce dramatic lighting effects.

Exterior Lighting

Your store front works for you at night too. In many communities, 50 percent more people pass store windows at night than in the daytime. Some store owners flood their entire facades with a striking "wash" of light. Every successful retailer constantly uses his window illumination to dramatize and attract

people who are passing by.

Neon lighting can be used for signing and to create subtle definitions. Increasingly popular exterior neon lighting is now used to surround individual show windows and "grab" more attention to the store front ▲74, 75, 76.

Show Window Lighting

Expect to see more lighting tracks installed on the vertical sides of closed-back show windows. The tracks are fitted to the vertical and overhead window frames depending on the needs of the store ▲78. Adjustable spotlights are attached to these tracks to light the front of books and merchandise. The fixtures can be

79 Above: ***Industrial fluorescent strip*** *lighting arranged in different planes, and angled in an overall concept with spot lighting on signs and focal points.* Noodle Kidoodle, Paramus, N.J.

80 Below: ***A compact, recessed, oblong fluorescent lighting fixture*** *evenly washes the walls from floor to ceiling of this medical book department.* UNIVERSITY BOOKSTORE, Madison, Wisc.

81 Above L: *Stylish indirect lighting fixtures* light the ceiling and balance the "commercial effect of parabolic lighting fixtures." Wall posters and step stools add to the "good feel" of the store. Books Inc., Palo Alto, Calif.

82 Above R: *Stagger pattern of recessed fluorescent lights* silhouettes vinyl letter messages applied to glass show windows. WORDSWORTH, Cambridge, Mass.

83 Below L: *Entrance vestibule* is illuminated by mid-lighting. MEDIA PLAY, Columbus, Ohio.

84 Below R: *Recessed squares of florescent lighting* in the entrance foyer and floating clouds of the main ceiling visually interact with strip and track lighting. MEDIA PLAY, Columbus, Ohio.

lamped with varying intensities of light to reinforce the mood and theme of a particular display. Window lighting may also originate from the bottom, like stage footlights, to throw light upward for everyday modeling effects or to create special (Halloween) shadow effects. Take care to protect access to the lamp and lighting fixtures from all customers, children in particular.

With special adapters almost any kind of decorative lighting fixture, chandelier, globes, and spotlights can be suspended from lighting tracks ▲111, 123, 139. Whenever possible, the source of window lighting should be positioned to light the front books and merchandise.

General Contrast Lighting

General lighting is often used to both highlight and contrast particular areas, items, or groups of items in show windows and the store. Books and other gift merchandise placed on a pedestal stand, in an armoire, or other prop can be accented with pinpointed spot lighting.

Contrast lighting should also be flexible. General contrast lighting can be especially useful in supporting seasonal and holiday DVM theme presentations. The addition of "color sleeves" to standard fluorescent lamps will change the color of light to match the color of the sleeve: red, yellow, orange, green. General interior lighting is often supplemented with feature and adjustable spot lights to dramatize display steps, end-caps, and strike zone display areas.

Color in Displays

People walking quickly or driving past a store front only retain a fleeting image of the display. They will react to the colors and lighting in a show window presentation well before they see the items displayed in it. Their conclusion is based purely on the appeal of the colors, the flash of light, and the announcements they have seen.

> Tip: Color combinations found on greeting cards are a wonderful source of simple ideas for everyday, Christmas, and seasonal color schemes.

Tips on Show Window Color Selection

When choosing colors for window displays, scale and proportion should also be considered. If the display is big, then you might want to reduce its mass. Dark wall colors will tend to shrink the size of the space. When the eye comes against a dark or strong shade, it shuts down. Conversely, light or pale shades give small display areas the perception of greater space and openness. Natural and artificial light can play odd tricks with colors. To get a handle on the color requirements of the window, determine which direction the window will face. Is the principle exposure north, south, east, or west? If the window is flooded with sunshine part of the day, there may not be any need for a bright, cheerful colored background. Too bright a color and artificial light in unusually sunny display areas have a tendency to make the space indistinct and hazy. If, however, the window or display area faces north, something warm and cheerful is needed. Sunny yellow color can arouse the sensation of sunlight in a dim area.

The Impact of Color on Scale and Proportion

There are many good books available on the subject of color. Here are a few ideas and tips to get you started with your show windows:

- Everyday use—Use neutral colors to coordinate with the interior store color scheme.
- Christmas—Polished gold and/or silver or red and/or green foil with snow flakes, candy canes, simulated snow, ornaments, and ribbons laced through the slots.
- Valentine's Day—Pink, lavender, or light green with ribbons, hearts, flowers, and vines entwined in the props.
- Mother's Day—Pink, melon, or green with ribbons and plants.
- Father's Day—Burnt orange, brown, and black with foam cutouts.
- Halloween—Black and orange, grey and white.

For very wide open–back window situations, consider alternating neutral colors (grey, beige, khaki, or white) for everyday appeal.

Accent and Historical Colors

For historical color themes, use deep-tone dependable colors (regimental red, blue, green, or gold). These colors are often used to create historical or other dramatic backgrounds for special themes. When you have arrived at the combination that will predominate, then introduce "accent colors." Often a sharp color can be used as an accent because it doesn't occur in large quantities. An accent color brings out the whole quality of a color scheme just as a seasoning does a salad. Therein lies a basic understanding of the display of books. Often the color of the book jacket or the product positioned in the display is the accent color.

Predicting Color Outcome

In window display, the color scheme means the use of colors and the various elements that go together to make a presentation like paint, the fabric, wallpaper, floor covering, furniture, and props. When you develop a color scheme, first choose the predominating colors the backgrounds will have. How do you know what color to use? Look at the best of the other stores in your area, whether they are bookstores or not. Then, consult your personal reaction in matters effected by the direction the outlet faces (sunlight and exposure) to the scale, proportion, and harmony.

Every kind of illusion can be produced with the imaginative use of colors. These things are risky and require considerable knowledge of the use of color. Sometimes you may need to experiment and may have to paint the space two or three times to get it right. There is a simple way for you to achieve the results you want while avoiding this calamity. Buy a small quantity of each color of paint you are considering. Paint the color onto large 36" pieces of white poster board. When the paint dries (it will change color as it dries), tape the painted color boards up on the wall you intend to paint. Check to see which shade of the color has the greatest appeal. This process can save you the frustration, time, and expense of painting an area several times.

A word of caution: don't overdo the color angle. That old saying, "Water, water everywhere and not a drop to drink," can be restated to read, "Color, color everywhere and not a spot to relax."

Well-signed and lighted multi-title display tables outsell cluttered and poorly lit displays by a considerable margin in most stores.

★ ★ ★ ★ ★

A comfortable knowledge of the things that can be done with color comes from the kind of training and experience few layman have. If you have a difficult color problem, get help locally if possible. If that doesn't work for you, see page 128.

Props, Furniture, and Accessories

5

It is impossible to cover every prop and its use in bookstore DVM in a single chapter. All of the display props created for use in the show window and interior of a bookstore call for some new effect or variation on an old one that could fill a book the size of the New York telephone book.

Many small and medium independent booksellers run their businesses in similar ways throughout the United States. The same is true in Britain and Australia. The way one store differs from the other deals with it's location, mix of titles, range of services, ambiance, layout, staff attitude, and image of the store, that is, the things that reflect the personality of its owner.

The interior look of a store and its visual presentation is a statement of what the owner wants the public to think of the store. Interior DVM props and displays can help bring the overall look of the store to life, by making the character and the image more convincing.

The Case for Props

Props are the odds and ends of articles that are used for DVM display purposes. Props can be divided into two classes: those that are used to accessorize and perk up a display, and those that are utilitarian.

The selection of the props is extremely important. A good prop contributes both to the eye appeal and the atmosphere of a display. A large room set should appear furnished and suggest that people really could live in and use it. The pictures, clocks, table top accessories (china, silver, glassware, cloth, and linen), flowers, plants, window backing, and lighting, must support the selling idea of the display.

Some props are difficult to obtain, while others easy. Everyday props can be easily purchased[2], and specialty props can be borrowed from large stores or rented from free-lance window trimmers. A tour of garage sales is one way to dredge up unique and quality items of furniture and accessory props at a modest cost if you have the space to store them. Ask around. Props can also be made, and almost all props can be refurbished and given a second life with a coat of spray paint.

Once you have the props, the trick is to decide how to put the various pieces together in a manner that will prove popular and attract customers into the store.

Book Props

Book props[3] are a natural addition to the ambiance of most bookstores ▲32. Sets of papier-mâché book props make wonderful devices to fill overstocked displays. Sets of false, lightweight books can be made

85 Left: *Gold foil panels* on the back wall reflect warm light and color into this festive entertainment theme window display. B&N, New York, N.Y.

by wrapping extra book jackets around styrofoam blocks, cut to the size of the particular title. If weight is not a concern, new jackets on old (nonreturnable books) of the same size are useful for converting overstock and building up quantities of hardbound window displays.

Food and Drink

With good food and drink props, it is not difficult to produce a display in which the food and drink (if any) look realistic and support the cooking and entertainment sections. Wonderful props of bread, French, Italian, and German, can be made by purchasing and then varnishing loaves of real bread. Wheat stalks, bagels, and hard rolls can be preserved by coating them with clear acrylic spray. Simulated dishes of fish, fowl, pasta, pizza, realistic grapes, fruits, and vegetables, are available from specialty prop makers. Glasses of tea are usually tea, coffee is coffee or a solution of brown sugar, and water is usually water.

Flowers

Flowers add to the atmosphere of a store. It is natural to find fresh flowers and plants in a bookseller's home. That is why many booksellers of "home" items think flowers should be seen in their stores ▲50, 80, 85.

Flowers are beautiful props that help create market separation and make one store different from its competition ▲66, 87. The use of plants is not a strategy for everyone, but in the right place, they work. Thousands of "real" poinsettias were used as the main Christmas decor by

Tower Books & Records ▲88, B&N, and Borders in 1995. Live plants have great mass market appeal.

Real flowers are important when customers can examine them closely. Artificial flowers, used in windows must look natural. The best artificial flowers are expensive but it is false economy to buy inferior ones. A good tip is to use real green foliage with artificial flowers. Expensive artificial flowers should always be handled with care as well as real ones. It is important that real plants are watered and changed regularly and that flowers be carefully arranged in their vases. Artificial flowers must be fire proof. Silk flowers and natural plants as well as metal plant sculptures should be hand dusted.

The choice of color and type of flower or plant that is chosen for a particular promotion is important. At Easter, lilies are appropriate, at Christmas, poinsettias, during the fall use chrysanthemums. Have your florist provide a recommended schedule of flowers of the month and submit an annual budget to provide and maintain plants at the entrance and strategic locations inside the store and café to boost late-night sales.

The small florist shop we designed into a large and busy bookstore was successful. All really large supermarkets have flower shops. Keep an eye open for potential development in this area ▲86. A flower shop in a bookstore may sound bizarre, but consider the Japanese bookstore that Youseff Antonio Nicoli showed me in Sao Paulo, Brazil. It included a live fish (sushi) market in the back of the store to meet

the needs of customers and it works! That's why the idea of selling flowers in a bookstore is not too far fetched.

Scenic Art Murals, Prints, Posters, and Pictures ▲89

As with other props, it is important that scenic art, prints, posters, and pictures you choose for your DVM program closely relate and support the themes and image of the store. Let's first deal with framed pictures, posters, and prints, Glass should be removed from picture frames, principally because it reflects light in display windows and also because it makes pictures appear heavy.

The use of pictures, posters, and prints in windows and inside the store is a reliable way of conveying any number of ideas and themes, which can include sports, travel, food, auto, boating, and countless others, each contributing an intriguing visual image.

Nordstroms' department stores set a cultural precedent in many of their stores by displaying framed original paintings by local artists that were consistent with the image of Nordstroms. Hung in appropriate locations, these paintings add to the decor, ambiance, and image of the store. Hanging these paintings provides an opportunity for Nordstroms' customers to see and buy original works of art. We understand Nordstroms collects a sales commission in the process. The point of the story is that quality original art is selected, shown, and sold in some of the best stores in America. Why not in yours?

Scenic art in the form of wall murals are appearing more

86 Above: *Flowers merchandised* in cart at entrance to airport shop. San Francisco International, Calif.

87 Above R: *We set the stairs back* to allow space for a warm, cozy atmosphere. This is a kind of personal sanctuary for quiet reading, reflecting, and mediation on all three levels. Natural light and plants are essential to the theme. BookPeople Bookstore & Café, Austin, Tex.

88 Below: *Poinsettias are natural props* that convey the spirit of peace and Christmas in most superstore chains. Tower Records, New York, N.Y.

frequently in independent and chain superstores. One new superstore recently provided an expansive mural in their children's department depicting the landscape of Old Santa Rosa, California, thereby integrating the whimsical tale of *James and the Giant Peach* by Roald Dahl. This art work was incorporated into the store DVM program to reinforce the store's image and quickly make the store part of the cityscape. Unique art was used to extend the outreach of this new store into the community. Whimsical murals of authors enjoying a cup of coffee with each other, murals of literary greats who have visited and signed books in the store, figures from *Chaucer's Canterbury Tales* are subjects found in scenic art that have appeared on the walls of cafés, children, and general book departments of some of our best stores. Scenic art, painted on canvas and hung in matched panels like wallpaper or painted directly on the walls of the store, can be a unifying means of tying the various visual elements of the store together. Art can by used to round out a store's image.

Props That Divide

Stores that serve the need of their literary communities, custom tailor their image with practical props that can also be used by its customers. Chairs, stools, tables, real (and player) pianos, wide aisles, clearly marked sections and shelves, working fireplaces, books on tape preview, and music listening stations are all props that support the store's ambiance. Child-sized theaters, and video and computer work-

stations are part of the inventory of practical in-store display and visual merchandising props available to booksellers.

Call them what you will—props, store fixtures, specialty fixtures, accessories—they are all props that can become important, high-visibility features of successful stores.

Off-the-Shelf Fixture Display Props

One of our favorite standard display fixtures are baker's racks,[4] and pasta carts. These are useful displays that can, for example, be used to tap into the lucrative, one-stop shopping market for coffee, coffee beans, personal espresso machines or sets of demitasse/espresso cups to compliment your café business. Yuppie communities and neighborhoods dense with artists and art lovers are reported to be active purchasers of coffee and coffee-related merchandise and probably a good place for a classy baker's rack.

Mirror Props

Mirrors can be hung in frames the same as pictures, but be careful about reflections. If you can't get rid of reflections by any other way, coat the glass with a solution of ordinary Epsom salts which are available from drug stores. The only way to check for reflections is to look at the window from every angle with the lights on.

Bread and Butter Props

If your store is actually engaged in show window display, bread and butter props will prob-

ably help you. Table 5 lists thirty–two items or versions of items we have seen used in some of the best bookstore DVM displays. The number next to the items indicate individual drawings of the props, and in some cases, individual photos of displays incorporating the prop. Open-top push carts with books and flowers have the power to attract attention and stop traffic.

Store Architecture and Design as Props

Whether it means designing and building a slick contemporary space or rehabilitating an existing building, store architecture and design are the mother of all props ▲95, 96, 128. In our experience bringing together the right mix of architecture and design is a time-consuming activity, yet it is critical to establishing and creating the right store image ▲1. It does not matter if the construction of the store requires restoring the art deco design of a building, replenishing original lighting fixtures, refurbishing wood floors and brass accents, and gold leafing the accent of restored columns, the design should strive to make the store a "one-of-a-kind place," a signature store that appeals to a wide variety of people through its ambiance, the appeal of its environment, and value-added services.

Making Props

The making of props is itself an art. Yet beginners can do a great deal when they are interested and willing to invest the time. Most props are made of wood, foam core, wire mesh, or

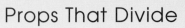

Props That Divide

Consider using screens, structures, and electronic equipment that are consistent with the store image as props to divide space and unify merchandising presentation.

89 Above: *Loggia style screen* designed with seats and listening station. MEDIA PLAY, Columbus, Ohio.
90 Left: *Store directory and video wall* introduce merchandise classifications and divide space. MEDIA PLAY, Columbus, Ohio.

Anatomy of a Festive Entertainment Theme
Imaginative setting employs numerous props.

Gold foil

Book jackets

Festive flower spray

Champagne bottle

Feature title

Wine glass

Party table cloth

Undercloth

Gift wrappings (removed)

Pink napkin

String of pearls

Face up book titles

Fruit ornament

Feature title

Dining chair upholstered red with tinsel

Corinthian column spray-painted gold

91 Left: *Asymmetrical multi-title* display in a closed-back window setting. B&N, New York, N.Y.

92 Left: *Large multi-subject* scenic art wall. B&N, New York, N.Y.
93 Above: *Frank White admiring portrait* of the store founder. Hugendubel Bucher, Frankfurt, Ger.

papier-mâché. Papier-mâché is made by boiling strips of newspaper in water until they are reduced to a pulpy paste, and then a solution of size (available from your local paint store) or white glue is added. The pulpy paste is then molded to a form desired. The shape is retained when it dries and hardens. When it has dried, the papier-mâché can be painted any color.

Finding the Help You Need

Two key words to retailing today are to "Ask around." Look for a window trimmer to help

94 Above: ***Portraits of the founder*** *at three stages of his career face the main open stairwell.*
95 Above R: ***Balconies*** *furnished with seats upholstered in primary colors and cantilevered beneath escalators.*
96 Bottom R: ***High-back****, booth type seating on lower level.* All; Hugendubel Bucher, Frankfurt, Ger.

create your window display. Expect to pay $60 to $170 per month to the trimmer. You can find a window trimmer by "asking around." Be sure to clarify the cost of the window trimming and labor versus the material and the cost of buying or renting props. Find out if the trimmer has props to rent. Work with the trimmer to develop your display schedule. Invest some time and money into scheduling and planning your displays.

Display Contests

Your efforts will provide instant gratification and boost

Table 5: Checklist of DVM Props

Atmosphere Pieces & Props:	Trees, arches, doors, windows, columns, pedestals, weather vanes.
Furniture Props:	Bookcases, chimney, tables, chairs, rockers, steps, ladders, folding screens, bean bags, children's items.
Rolling Props:	Wheelbarrows, carts, wagons, train baggage carts, automobiles and parts, taxis, busses, bicycles.
Sports Props:	Seasonal equipment, uniforms, posters, photographs.
People Props:	Live people, mannequins, animation, and costumed characters with tie-in merchandise, plush animals.

Table 6: Checklist of Architectural Element Props

Doors:	Solid paneled entrance doors in frames (available in a variety of sizes).
Frames and Pediments:	Glass doors with panes as room dividers. Use pediments with sign panels and center floor dividers.
Windows:	Available in a variety of widths to create show window and center floor backing.
Fireplace Mantels:	Used in windows and center floor to provide more ledges for featuring book titles, potbelly stoves, bricks, stone, slate.

Table 7: Props to Raise Things Up

Natural cedar & birch risers	Platforms	Easels
Wood cubes	Risers and U-bends	Banners
Crates and barrels	Molded cinder blocks	Banner stands
Tub baskets	Ladders	Trellises
	Tri-level tables	Pedestals

Table 8: Things That Join and Hold Things Together

Punch clips	Slatwall	Special hooks
Ceiling clips	Foam core	Dress-maker pins
Magic hang-ups	Gator board	Bulletin sign holders
Ceiling anchor magnets	Hercules clips	Hanging acrylic sign
Ceiling grills	Toggle bolts	holder

Table 9: Natural and Regional Theme Props

Grass	NAUTICAL THEMES	Canoes
Grass blankets	Fishnet	Paddles
Grapevines	Rope	Oars
Snow trees	Crates	Beach chairs
Snow branches	Treasure chests	DESERT THEMES
Snow/Snowflakes	Fish	Giant rocks
Icicles	Starfish/Crabs/Shrimp	Wagon wheels
Snow shovels	Lobster traps	Hay bales
Bags of salt/deicer	Corks	Sand
Bags of sand	Wicker furniture	Cactus
Bamboo poles	Boats	Wood chips
Natural birch poles		
Giant size urns		

Table 10: Props and Things That Move

Wheelbarrows	Tugboat	Satellite
Wheels	Skow	Space station
Trucks	Autos	Space shuttle
Airplane	Trains	Wagons
Sailboat	Fire engines	Ceiling fans
Ship	UPS truck	Porch swing

Table 11: Props to Build and Support Store Atmosphere

Rope lights	Flags	Seamless paper
Fabrics	Banners	Signs - Natural
Tablecloths	Styrofoam sheets	Signs - Neon
Pennants	Styrofoam balls	Video
Bunting - Fans	Food/Bread/Pasta	Ribbons

Table 12: Store Furniture and Specialty Fixture Props

SEASONAL	Garlands	BACK TO SCHOOL
Tinsel trees	Christmas trees	Giant crayons
Tinsel branches	Yule tree lights	Giant pencils
Holly	Desk telephones	Answering machine
Wreaths	Straw baskets	Calculator
Gift wrapped basket		Computer keyboards
		Video monitors

97 Above: **Children's** *brightly colored software demonstration station.* Noodle Kidoodle, Paramus, N.J.
98 Below: **Face-out presentation**, *color, graphics, and promotional displays help make this a pleasant and friendly store.*
ZANY BRAINY, Newark, Del.

99 Left: **Wide, easy-rising stair** *connects three floors of the store.* BookPeople Bookstore and Cafe, Austin, Tex.
100 Above: **Store architecture as a prop.** *Georgian colonial entrance to the scholarly book department.* Charlesbank Books & Café, Boston, Mass.
101 Below: **Study sketch** *of a music department.* KWA project in work.

Music

CD HITS   CD   SINGLES   COMPACT DISCS   FAMILY FAVORITES

Classical

First Level: CD / Tape Wall Display
with Feature Entrance to the
Classical, Jazz & Blues Music Department

Plan

102 Left: *Cutout half-life-size prop* characters add to fantasy theme of this exceptional comic book store interior. Universal Walk, Los Angeles, Calif.

103 Above: *Space theme* in ceiling and graphic elements. B. Dalton, Annapolis, Md.

104 Below: *Frank White with Bionic Bob's head* which is under consideration for an interactive store directory. Frankfurt Book Fair, Ger.

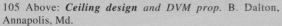

106 Above: *A prop fixture that divides space.* To help close the sale, CD's are stacked and available at the point of demonstration. KWA Design study for music preview station.

105 Above: *Ceiling design* and DVM prop. B. Dalton, Annapolis, Md.

107 Below: *Ledge merchandising* on high center children's fixtures used as space dividers. Borders Books and Music, Phoenix, Ariz.

sales and customer recognition. Many publishers conduct display contests periodically to promote new titles. Many of these contests provide cash and free trip rewards. More importantly, for the store to win a display contest adds to staff confidence, adds to the prestige of the store, and to its standing in the trade.

In chapter 1 we learned that there are many places in the store that can be used as focal points to generate customer interest and improve traffic flow. Display merchandising that focuses the seven strategic areas of the store will add to the "good feeling" of the store and overall sales volume.

Props help to make customer contact.
Props help customize presentations.

Props are essential for innovation and presentation.

Props make communication simpler and more effective.

★ ★ ★ ★ ★

Part 2 of this book follows. It focuses on trends, merchandising techniques, and DVM improvisation in action.

Part 2

Merchandising the Walls

6

More visible stock is found shelved on the perimeter walls of the typical small bookstore than in the center of the space. In addition to holding some of the bulk of the stock titles and sideline items, walls have two other main purposes. They provide spaces for extra overstock and spaces for display. The quantity of stock displayed on wall shelving is often increased by adding shelving sections above the normal seven-foot height of standard wall store fixtures. The additional shelving capacity gained provides a place for the display and overstock area. Overstock area is the place where extra copies of slow-moving titles and extra copies of important books are stored (right at hand in the overstock space) during busy selling seasons ▲109.

Display

In a self-service store, most wall displays are classified as a "general" display or a special "eye-stopping wall focal point" display. There is no formal definition of a focal point, but ours is *"the place within a wall display that captures the attention of the customer through the use of a 'break' in the top line of the store fixture."* In our view, a true focal point is a vertical display that breaks through the valance of the wall store fixture. As seen in illustration ▲108 the normal wall display goes up to the valance, while the center section of wall cases continues through the valance to the ceiling. The customer's eye responds to this discontinuous line, and make the focal point a powerful attention getter. If you have no need for overstock capacity, narrow slatwall panels can be added to create a display in a specific area or around the perimeter of the store. This provides an opportunity for a variety of display applications, but it requires a lot of inventory and a lot of work to maintain.

A wall display makes a benefit statement to customers. It tells them what categories of merchandise are offered in that part of the store. Book assortments displayed on the walls should provide strong category definition and relate to the bulk of the stock. Since book stores use both category presentation and focal points, a variety of fixtures may be needed to accommodate these divergent requirements, such as slatwall fixture adaptors and a variety of shelving types.

Several points to remember:

1. At each focal point selected for display, there should be one merchandise statement, left to right, top to bottom, in the display.
2. Wall displays should be changed frequently to keep them new and add excitement to the store on a regular basis.

108 Left: ***Pictogram** art, category signs, and lighted face-out inserts support the merchandising concept of this successful children's store.* UBS Kids, Madison, Wisc.

Chapter 6

Think Wall Cases and T-Walls

Many European booksellers have for years focused their attention on merchandising wall sections. That focused interest is reflected in the layout and ambiance of their stores. Putting emphasis on wall section merchandising is an idea that is slowly picking up steam in the United States. We find wall merchandising used more and more in independent and chain super bookstores and particularly in (British) corporate-owned airport shops located in the United States. There is also a renewed interest in T-walls, wall cases that intersect the perimeter casework system of the store by United States booksellers.

The reason for the shift toward extensive use of T-walls is to create added capacity shops within shops, rooms within rooms ▲110, and departments within departments. In those concepts, wall cases arranged in back-to-back relationships are used to create divisions of space.

T-walls create more attractive book corners and alcoves where book browsers can lose themselves, create distinctive settings for important departments, and provide more space for end-cap merchandising ▲61. The open space surrounded by these T-wall systems is frequently merchandised with flat-top tables, gondolas, seating, or other specialty type merchandising equipment. That's a lot of flexibility for a lowly T-wall case.

Comparative Merchandising Features of Wall Cases

Wall cases are depended upon to display every imaginable kind of edition from the top to the bottom of each wall section to it's fullest advantage. There are several ways to achieve positive results.

The first and one of the least expensive methods is to slant the entire wall case fixture back against the wall at an angle. This design will permit light to strike the face of all the titles on the shelves in the section. Slant-back wall fixtures are favored by many super chain bookstores ▲121. The slant-back display approach does not take up too much valuable floor space.

The second system employs minimal width (front to back) wall cases, with each shelf angled for viewing and adjustable for height. Flat shelves are used at the top of the fixtures (where it is important for titles to face straight out, rather than on an angle, away from the customer). Flat shelves are also used to hold a variety of DVM inserts ▲108. Inserts are important for the face out viewing of maps, children's, soft cover and pamphlet type books, monograms, games, and software. Vertical inserts made with a narrow band slatwall are important to display hang-up, blister-pack type merchandise and other hangables right in the shelving section, adjacent to similar titles. "Push outs" are another type of insert used to "push" small books to the front of deep shelves. Step shelf inserts are useful to display tape cassettes and small children's books. Special T-shelves can be reversed for the stocking of software and games.

The third basic approach to the design of wall section shelving uses a half angle bottom, straight top wall case concept ▲66. This type of case is ideal when you have lots (maybe too much) space and the cost of fixtures and fixture transportation are not the deciding factors. The fourth approach utilizes a low, wide ledge base case with narrow overshelves for reserve stock and flat-top stack space ▲107, 111. High-ledge bases provide a space to examine Bibles, art, technical, and reference books, with overshelves for stock and display ▲122.

Commercial and custom wall store fixtures are made of wood, metal, and various composition boards. The colors and finishes of wall store fixtures selected are critical to the DVM mission. Wall cases are depended on to provide graphic category signing, shelf labeling, sometimes lighting, and always the flexibility to integrate a vast assortment of sizes and types of hard, soft bound, and flex cover traditional books, audio and video, music, CD's, and prerecorded tapes, packaged coffee and tea, and textile and gift sidelines ▲134 - 138.

Impact of Variety

The natural enemy of merchandise excitement is monotony. Stacks and stacks of books and merchandise on fixtures, and shelf after shelf of merchandise on a gondola run can be extremely boring. For this reason it becomes important to create variety through height planning ▲60. Keep in mind there are other means to achieve variety through presentation techniques and fixture selection.

It is useful at this point to think of the store as a kind of theater where the front of the store is at the lowest level while the rest of the store unfolds and builds higher towards the sides and back. This provides a "system" to the variety of heights and creates design continuity. Height variety, for the sake of variety does not serve the purpose of "variety impact." To achieve variety impact there must be a balance in heights as well as a balance in fixture types (not such an enormous variety of fixtures that there is a sense of confusion to the store). The stores pictured in this guide represent this concept. It makes the stores not only appear organized, but helps the customer understand how the store is organized by systematizing the variety.

Rolling Ladders

High wall cases and overstock areas are best accessed with rolling ladders fastened to a continuous metal track attached to the wall sections. Rolling ladders provide physical access to load and unload stock onto the overstock shelves. They add ambiance and a library look to the store ▲26, 66, 109.

> Tip: Provide a neat sign attached to a step on the ladder at eye level to read "Staff Use Only." These notices serve to discourage customers from climbing up the ladders.

High Center Floor Wall Cases

Center floor space divisions of T-walls can be arranged at any logical point in the store that takes into consideration the requirements of customer and product traffic, circulation, visibility, security, and other practical matters. They may be arranged in a T, X, or an L form to create a comfortable and appropriate background for linguistics, history, art, collectibles to just about any classification you choose ▲61, 80. There are dozens of possibilities, even in the smallest store. Now that we have the tools, let's merchandise the walls.

Merchandising General Book Wall Sections

Wall section merchandising starts by first adjusting shelves to provide minimum clearance for the tallest book on each shelf. If the section has a limited number of over size titles, these should be placed at the beginning or end of the section. Next, stock is spread evenly from bottom to top with current best-sellers and important new titles faced out for quick customer identification.

After the best-sellers and new titles are faced out, continue to face out less important titles until each shelf has the maximum number of face outs.

The shelves at eye level should have the highest number

109 Below: *Rolling ladders are practical for reaching high overstock. They are also a wonderful visual prop.* Kepler's Books & Magazines, Menlo Park, Calif.

110 Right: **Wood walls** *with category signage, shelved end-caps, and overstock. Banners in a high ceiling create a spacious ambiance.* Harry W. Schwartz, Milwaukee, Wisc.

111 Bottom L: **High wall cases** *with angled shelves, overstock shelves, category signage, and flat-base display ledge.* DILLON'S, London, U.K.

112 Bottom R: **High wood T-wall unit** *with slatwall end-caps and free standing category signage.* BookPeople Bookstore & Café, Austin, Tex.

of face out titles.

For wall sections with an extremely large quantity of stock, select and leave one or two copies of slow-moving titles spine out, and place the balance into the appropriate overstock. This will create space and allow best-sellers and important titles to be faced out. Caution should be exercised to maintain POS (point-of-sale) control on titles taken out so that sales are not lost by stock being in overstock and not on the shelf. For wall sections with limited stock, distribute books and face outs evenly on every shelf to fill up the section.

A limited number of wall sections will contain hardcover, trade paper, and mass market titles on a particular subject because of strong customer interest and because impact would be lost if they were displayed in two separate areas. Special inserts are provided in certain wall sections to accommodate the face out display of soft bound titles which are integrated with adjoining hard bound stock.

Art Section Merchandising

This area requires special attention because the majority of titles are expensive and oversized. Merchandising this section follows the basic bottom-to-top technique discussed in merchandising the wall section.

It is obviously not practical to mylar wrap each and every art title; however, in this section, for some stores, it is almost imperative that some of the titles be wrapped due to the expense of the books involved. Such a section is, of course, the art sec-

113 Above: *High director chairs for customers to preview overhead video movie display.* MEDIA PLAY, Columbus, Ohio.
114 Above R: *Wall graphics in strip holders above pro-tech gondolas. Floor is patterned and stained concrete.* UPSTART CROW BOOKSTORE, Los Angeles, Calif.

tion. Customers will certainly refuse to buy an art book if it is in any way mishandled and has not been dealt with delicately. Furthermore, a mylar-wrapped cover does tend to subconsciously tell the customer that you value the book. He/she is likely, therefore, to value it as well. During the Christmas season, where space permits, the three or four most important new art books (in their jackets) should be placed at eye level for easy examination and to provide maximum exposure for the books.

There are many different types of presentation for expensive large format art books. One of the favored is ledge base fixtures. The wide base ledge permits face-up display of large titles below the ledge top and adds a flat ledge for stacking and examination of the titles. Space above the ledge should be adequate for four rows of full-face display. Ledge presentation will allow for stacking quantities of the same title during busy seasons. Space below the ledge (behind the vertical facing) can be used for overstock of important books where it's needed. Locked wood doors can be added to create secured overstock space. If one or more sections of the wall presentation are modest in width, glass doors can be introduced to secure very expensive ($1500 and up) art books. Clear glass doors and proper lighting will

Third Level: North Wall Software / Multimedia Display

115 Above: *Design study for children's software* and multimedia display. KWA, Columbus, Ohio.

116 Below: *Design study for divider wall* in children's department. KWA Columbus, Ohio.

DVM design studies such as these, as well as ▲ 20, 101, and 128 are made to visualize the selling situation before construction begins. At KWA we find these studies to be essential in communicating how we propose to incorporate our "client's ideas" into their stores. DVM visuals are a way to insure that everyone is "playing off the same sheet of music."

permit these books to be seen. Hand selling will fulfill the examination and sales closing requirements.

Moderately priced art books can be presented on ladder type displays with acrylic holders (which interchange with large format calendars and remainder books). Quality stacks of remainder art titles are generally best sold on whales.

Merchandising Children's Books ▲103

The children's section is one of the most demanding areas to merchandise and maintain in the entire store, but if done correctly it can create an atmosphere of excitement as well as additional sales at the registers ▲115, 116.

Each section in the juvenile area requires a slightly different display approach; baby and pixie books are long, short, thin, thick, flimsy, and come in every shape and color. Arrange the books by size, shape, and series. For example, put the "Clock Book," "Telephone Book," and others together. Group the "Pop-Ups," the "I Am a Puppy," "I Am a Rabbit," series and the "Touch and Feel" books.

A full children's book department will require the same variety of wall cases and displays and DVM techniques as a freestanding children's store ▲97. Low, ledge type base cases ▲107, (similar to those used in the art department) are of value in presenting story books and picture books. Angled and adjustable shelves, sometimes mounted onto slatwalls can provide decorative backgrounds for DVM presenta-

tions. This flexibility permits an easy interchange of hard and soft bound books, plush toys, and novelties.

Workbooks, activity, and color books are best displayed face out in shelf inscrts, preferably lighted, and seven to nine rows high ▲98, 130. Classics and picture books are generally shelved six rows high. Series books are shelved seven to nine rows high ▲170. Special high children's wallcases and inserts can be ordered to accommodate as many as thirteen rows ▲118.

We agree with many merchandisers who believe the use of mobiles, flags, and plush props are essential to creating ambiance in the children's department.

This large department should allocate space for teacher's aids and supplies. Service desks are

117 Above: ***Merchandising children's books.*** Southern Oregon State College, Ashland, Oreg.
118 Above Right: ***Boxcar prop*** *on theme table with end cubes in a children's department.* Tattered Cover Bookstore, Denver, Colo.

sometimes built into wall case systems surrounded with merchandise that leaves adequate space for the staff to move behind the counter during busy times. This is essential. Other DVM features of the children's service desk include provision for gift wrapping, shelves for storing special orders, and merchandising space for stickers, rubber stamps, and related sidelines ▲137.

Don't fret about high ceilings in children's selling space. High ceilings provide the opportunity for skylights, transom lights, fans, banners, flags, live plants, weather vanes, towers, and castles. Other DVM props, such as an aquarium ▲126, trains, and trucks, that children can sit in, lean on, and climb over, and pews, benches, and rocking chairs for parents and grandparents ▲157, work tables, stools, and children's furniture sets ▲148, picnic tables and benches

▲119, giant crayons ▲120, pencils, erasers, computer work stations, music listening stations, and the like are great image-building features and props for the department.

Merchandise the section by adjusting shelves from the bottom up so the tallest book on each shelf just fits. Next, face out titles starting from the bottom and working up, making sure that each shelf has about the same number of face outs. Picture books also come in a variety of sizes and are arranged by subject and, within each subject, by author.

Flats are displayed face out in special inserts within regular wall fixtures (on gondolas and tables) to feature title merchandise. The top-selling flats should be vertically displayed face out and at eye level. When flats are displayed in wall sections, position the titles so they have color-contrasted covers (large over-

size flats are displayed in large waterfall type fixtures on casters) ▲147.

Series books are merchandised by putting each series together and, if the series is numbered, arranged by number. To maximize sales, put the best selling series first, such as "Baby Sitter Club," "Boxcar Kids," followed by "Nancy Drew," then "Hardy Boys," and so on. Face out as many titles as possible on each shelf, especially the shelves at eye level.

Children's paperbacks are merchandised alphabetically by author. Shelves should be adjusted bottom to top so all titles stand up and face outs of top sellers are spread equally on each shelf. Avoid stocking "spineless" paperbacks but spine out wherever possible.

Health, exercise, poetry, music, religion, nature books, death, and science, are arranged by subject and by author within the sub-

119 Right: **Mom works with kids at children's table** and chair set. Waterfall display of activity books at left is easy to read. MEDIA PLAY, Columbus, Ohio.

120 Lower L: **Face-out presentation of videos** and an interactive video display set into a giant crayon located between two low gondolas with face-out presentation. Golden Book Shop, Universal Walk, Los Angeles, Calif.

121 Lower R: **Bibles and inspirational books** are displayed on the back wall, T-walls, and tables of this department. BOOKS-A-MILLION, Daytona Beach, Fla.

ject. Merchandising is the same as for other sections.

Children's music, video, computer software and hardware, plush games, and toys are merchandised with books to add importance to this department ▲21. The result will be that more human space will be needed to provide a high level of customer comfort. Typically, more in-store events are staged in the children's department than in any other one.

DVM color concepts for the children's section vary from "natural" wood looks ▲118, to bright colors with lots of white ▲117. Highly descriptive category signs like "Things That Move," are important and appreciated by customers.

Yes, the children's section requires more attention than most other sections. It should have one or more people assigned to maintain and see that it is well merchandised. Staff assignments in the children's section should be rotated so the entire staff can effectively merchandise the section, find requested titles, answer telephone inquiries, and make suggestions to customers ◆104.

Bibles

Bibles require special merchandising because

1. the independent bookstore's stock selection will consist of many different versions, each requiring distinct display separation from the others, so as to assist the customer visually in locating his/her desired version; and
2. bibles are packaged in various sizes and ways (hardbound, paperback, and boxed), thus requiring traditional and nontraditional methods of display.

122 Above: **Boxed, shrink-wrapped, and open Bibles** *are featured in this large department. Ledge fixtures provide space to examine titles and merchandise sets of Bible indexing tabs, highlighters, covers, and magnifiers. The church pew for seating is a nice touch.* Tattered Cover Bookstore, Denver, Colo.

Merchandising this section follows the basic bottom-to-top technique discussed in the merchandising of the wall section. In addition, two basic display rules must be followed:

1. Group by version: King James Version, Revised Standard Version, New English Bible, New American Bible, Living Bible, others.
2. Group within versions by use: Teachers, Reference.

You will notice the photograph shows that these two basic rules can be adhered to, whether your display space is large or small. By following the example given, each of your customers would find his or her section, and all styles available in that section would be at hand for their inspection ▲122.

The ledge-type fixture pictured provides the place to examine Bible titles. Church pews make good props in this section. Merchandise Bible book covers, stick-on Bible tabs, and highlighters, along with the book titles. Christian bookstores also merchandise choir robes and church supplies adjacent to the department ▲134.

Magazines

Magazines are carried in many stores to increase store traffic and impulse sales. When space is limited, magazines are best merchandised on wall store fixtures with twelve to fifteen rows of display pockets, arranged in three lighted tiers, and with key title merchandised at eye level. Often magazine fixtures are designed with a flat bottom ledge to display large quantities of single titles and newspapers. When more space is available full front merchandising is preferred ▲123. This idea of featuring every facing takes more space, but it can be more effective in high-traffic locations. Magazine inserts can be used on end-caps ▲124, in gondolas, and wall sections to feature specialty sections such as psychology, medical, business, computer, and multimedia magazines within the category. Large bulk display quantities of magazines require heavy duty dividers to keep the stock neat and orderly.

For small, independent stores, we have designed neat wall fix

123 Above: *Acclaimed one of the best merchandised newsstands* in America, this shop features all magazine titles face out. Hudson News, La Guardia Airport, New York, N.Y.
124 Left: *Low end-cap magazine merchandiser.* University Bookstore, Tokyo, Japan.
125 Below: *Well-stocked display stand* with newspapers, greeting cards, maps, and post cards. Hudson News, Regional Airport, Baltimore, Md.

126 Left: **An aquarium is placed on the bottom shelf** of this nature department wall case facing the children's section. Webster Books, Ann Arbor, Mich.
127 Center: **Children's computer station** with six monitors. Learningsmith, Cambridge, Mass.
128 Bottom: **Design study for an art,** photography, and architecture department. Lower face-out level is the front of doors to conceal overstock. KWA, Columbus, Ohio.

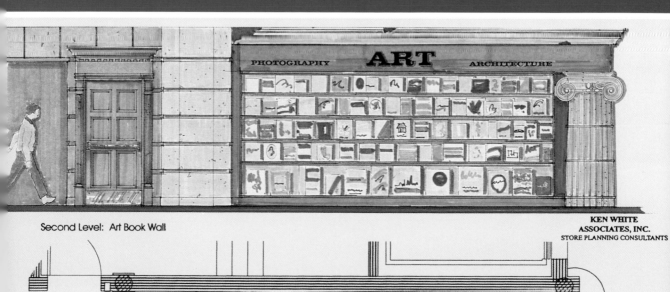

Second Level: Art Book Wall

PHOTOGRAPHY   **ART**   ARCHITECTURE

KEN WHITE ASSOCIATES, INC.
STORE PLANNING CONSULTANTS

Plan

129 Right: **Limited editions** *are displayed behind hinged glass doors.* Liberties Fine Books and Music, Boca Raton, Fla.

130 Lower L: **Demonstration models** *variety in fixturing and merchandise adds to casual attraction.* Learningsmith, Cambridge, Mass.

131 Lower R: **Light cove washes light** *on wall above mid-height, ledge-type children's wall book cases. The top ledge makes a neat home for plush toys and animals.* Borders Books and Music, Phoenix, Ariz.

132 Above: *Video monitor*, *changeable and dimensional posters and plaques are among the many props that help customers focus their interest on merchandise.* MEDIA PLAY, Columbus, Ohio.

133 Left: *A big red apple adds humor to the teacher's center sign.* Noodle Kidoodle, Paramus, N.J.

134 Below L: *Choir robes on center floor display.* Family Bookstore, Elk Grove Village, Ill.

135 Below R: *This T-shirt display is simple, neat, and well organized.* Airport Shop, Charlotte, N.C.

136 Above L: **Design study for travel theme** to be used in overstock wall cases. KWA, Columbus, Ohio.
137 Above R: **Kids T-shirts** displayed above wallcases on mannequins cut out of fibre board. The top wall shelf is merchandised with well-lighted plush. UPSTART CROW BOOKSTORE, Los Angeles, Calif.
138 Below: **Built-up table stock** merchandising with lighted wall cases. WATERSTONES Booksellers, London, U.K.

ture sections to combine face-out best-seller, mass market books, magazines, newspapers, local maps, postal, and greeting card items. Magazines grouped by subject are easy to shop and enjoy repeat business. When space is limited, the quantity of magazines to be merchandised can be increased by partially overlapping one face over the other. This technique reduces the amount of each facing seen by the customer but it does allow for a wider selection of titles, which may be more important in your location.

If stocked, adult magazines

are usually located on the highest row with only the top exposed.

Newspapers

Many customers depend upon their local bookstores for their daily and Sunday newspapers. Newspapers can generate significant drop-in traffic and stimulate weekend impulse and café sales. There is a trend to combine and market local, national, English, and foreign language newspapers. The type of fixture used depends upon the volume and variety of newspapers that will be stocked and the size and location of the stores ▲125. Attractive clear acrylic newspaper displays can be made with swivel casters and easily rolled into the best traffic location early in the morning when business is brisk.

Overstock Display

Overstocks are a vital element in developing the total floor-to-ceiling, "store full of books" image. Effective merchandising is as critical here as in any other part of the store.

Consider this strategy. Consolidate your stock for eight or nine months of the year and leave the top row open for overstock merchandising with stock posters, plush, props, and oversize titles. Then replace the overstock space with new stock at busy times.

The key to successful merchandising the overstock area is to keep the overstock shelf sections full of merchandise or props at all times. This will require creativity and time spent weekly merchandising the overstock either by building new displays or by changing titles or props to make old displays look new. Creativity is required because stock levels fluctuate throughout the year.

Large quantities of a title should not be put in overstock just to fill it up when this same quantity can be effectively displayed on the floor to generate additional sales.

Those bookstores that operate with POS inventory control systems will find that their overstock space is nearly empty most of the year. The DVM job is to keep these nearly empty, high-overstock wall sections "looking good" and making sure they contribute to the selling themes taking place in the store—a challenge by any stretch of the imagination.

Walls provide essential stock display space.

Walls offer a unique opportunity to get the customers' attention through the use of focal points.

★ ★ ★ ★ ★

We have seen the importance of walls and their role in the overall merchandising display of the store. Let us now see how center floor fixtures can be merchandised to fill their critical role in the success of the store.

Merchandising
Front and Center
Floor Display Fixtures

7

First Sell the Image

The purpose of the show windows and store front is to sell your image, attract customers' attention, and draw them into the store. Once the customer is inside, the next step is to put interior DVM strategies to work. The strategy for the interior display is to continue selling the image and to sell the merchandise.

Store fixtures are needed in bookstores to support and present a variety of cubical products, often heavy in weight and varied in size. Customers rank ease of shopping, good layout, and a comfortable environment high on their list of priorities. These priorities are followed by the perception of value, a knowledgeable staff, and a large selection of books.[2] That is why the proper use of fixtures throughout the store is so important. In this chapter we focus on attention-grabbing displays for tables, steps, gondolas, end caps, towers, and other fixtures that are designed to get the customers' attention to help sell the image of the store and move merchandise.

Aisle Merchandising

Think of the inside of the store as being divided into three areas linked by the main customer aisle. Area 1 consists of the store front, cash wrap, theme tables, and whales. Area 2 is the center of the store where gondolas are usually found. Area 3 will be the information counters, children's, or another specialty section with their whales, tables, gondolas and end-caps.

Because of its function, the aisle has the greatest amount of customer exposure and offers booksellers unlimited opportunities to maximize on current trends, customer interest, and seasonal events by timely and ever-changing displays of new, bestselling, and key backlist titles, cards, wrappings, and other sidelines. The choice of which product to stock will depend on the marketing focus of the store.

New-Arrival Displays and Theme Tables

Customers expect to find new-arrival and theme tables full and well merchandised in the front of the store. These displays are often built on open front tables and tables with front step down displays. Needless to say, continued movement of stock on and off the new arrival table is absolutely essential to highlight those books that have just arrived in stock. It is important to continually emphasize to the public that there is always something new in the bookstore.

139 Left: **Wicker baskets** and face-up merchandising of sale and bargain books marketed in a show window setting. Kepler's Books & Magazines, Menlo Park, Calif.

1.   Timing - It is critical that displays go up when customer interest is developing and that they are carried through until interest has diminished. Consult publishers, distributors, wholesalers, advertising, and display bulletins, and author tour schedules for theme table subjects and timing.

2.   Title Selection - This is important because not only are new and bestselling titles featured, but lesser known, related titles are merchandised around them to broaden the title selection which increases the probability of additional sales.

Some stores with limited floor space feature new arrival titles in high wall cases ▲10. New-arrival titles are also presented on increasingly popular whales, (special fixtures that combine the features of tables and front step down displays) ▲8, 19, 140.

Theme tables throughout the store should display and highlight titles which are merchandised in that particular section of the store. For example, if space permits, use a general theme or a group of books by one author on one table, at the store front, or in a specialty department.

If space is available, special theme tables can be coordinated with window displays and signs referring the customer to every major department. There, good selections of books pertaining to one general subject, such as business, cooking, art, reference, religion, multimedia, and children's are usually well received by customers.

Solid-top gondolas are often used to provide premium DVM locations in appropriate parts in the store. Solid wood tops are needed to support the weight of book displays. For gifts and novelties, glass tops support top level merchandise and allow light to filter to the lower shelves ▲114.

Theme table displays in the children's area are often smaller, equipped with casters, and are easily movable. Bright color tops are often used to support the display of bestsellers, new arrivals, and trend merchandise. The signing and display construction is the same as for adult theme tables.

Multi-Titled Table Display

The concept of collecting a selection of books by one writer/author from several parts of the store, also applies to collecting the work of several authors whose new titles are focused on a single subject. Hanging banner type signs over multi-titled displays helps catch customers attention ▲140 a. Prepare the store for these events by installing barnacle hooks on the ceiling tile tracks. These hooks permit banners and signs to be quickly hung from the ceiling. In the absence of tracks, install screw eyes in the main ceiling (with toggle bolts if needed) or use easily changed magnetic clip holders ▲32. Many of these inexpensive, well-designed devices are unobtrusive. We usually plan adjustable low-voltage, high-output lighting fixtures at these same locations to highlight and dramatize the signage and book titles offered in the display ▲32. Time and again we

have seen impressive sales results from the basic combination of a meaningful selling message on a well-planned sign above an important presentation of timely book titles.

Multi-title displays are used to capitalize on current customer interest and encompasses the merchandising of current bestsellers (hardcover and paperback) with lesser known, related titles. The process of presentation follows the same rules as the best-seller tables.

Best-Sellers and Mass Market Books

Effective merchandising of these classifications is critical because of the rapid turnover and the constant arrival of important titles. The titles selected for this area provide flexibility to change the front appearance of the store based on the movement of titles.

For wider stores, floor displays at the center entrance should contain the very newest arrivals, the most trendy titles at the time. Because of their visibility, these floor displays are probably the best way to draw people deeper into the store. It is therefore important that they be kept timely and are frequently changed. If you are moved to use dump type displays, consider

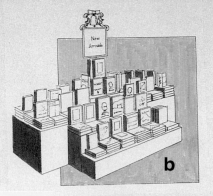

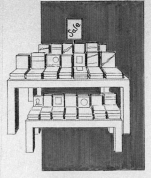

140 Right: *New-arrival and theme tables.*
*a: basic step unit; b: front basic step
with standard table and end stacker
boxes; c: open leg parsons type table;
d: rear view of "a" but empty; e: rear
view of "a" when loaded with understock tabletop display and promotional sign.*

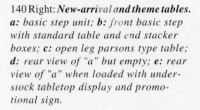

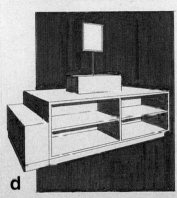

using permanent type dumps with title-coordinated headers. There should be only one title per floor display column, and they should be provided with title-coordinated headers.

Permanent type, single title racks may be used to display the top ten bestselling titles at the entrance and down the main aisle, particularly when these racks are displayed one title per fixture with a backup capacity.

We believe in vertical column merchandising because it allows the customer to see a full face presentation of the ten top fiction titles at once. It makes each one dynamically interact so that every book helps to display and sell the others. As with all store front area displays, it is absolutely essential that these titles be updated weekly.

Theme Tables

Theme tables are used to display new and bestselling titles that reflect current trends, customer interest, and seasonal events. Maximum productivity is achieved by proper timing and title selection ▲140 c.

Many successful booksellers constructed these theme displays in the basic step-down pyramid pattern, with the theme best-sellers highlighted by their position at the peak and center of the display ▲140 b, c, e. A broad selection of related titles and appropriate props are positioned around them.

For large stores, table understock merchandising is an integral and important part of the display because it contributes to the total visual image. Stacker boxes are sometimes used on the aisle side of the table to feature additional copies of new and best-selling titles.

The display is built by positioning the most aggressively purchased titles in the center of the table ▲140 e. Titles are placed horizontally to the front of the tables with dust jacket spines facing front and sloping down on both sides. The next horizontal row on both sides off the center row are stepped down from it and the same is done for the remaining rows until the front and back edges of the table are reached. Titles are now faced out on the center row by using book rests. Titles on the next front row are faced out by propping them against the center row. Caution should be taken not to obscure titles when facing out the lower

141 Left: ***Mass market gondola*** *with slatwall end-cap. Shelves are evenly space with 1/2-inch clearance above the books.*
142 Center: ***Trade reference gondola.*** *Shelves are adjusted to fit the average size while the tallest books are placed on the top shelf.*
143 Right: ***Professional and technical, or pro-tech, gondola*** *features new arrivals on end-caps. All three photos PSS Bookstore, Yokosuka, Japan.*

rows. In this type of display try to face out about 30 percent of your titles. On the aisle side of the table, use stacker boxes ▲140 e, or acrylic merchandisers to emphasize the bestselling titles. Merchandise the table's front side understock area with best-sellers and/or important new titles. These should be placed so that the majority of space behind them cannot be seen. The rear of the understock box can be used for normal stock ▲140 e. Stores with limited tables will have to display two or three themes on a single table with display construction identical to a single theme table.

Whales

The versatility of whales permits all of the front and understock to be seen and available in a more aggressive fashion on both sides than on tables and ends. Title content should be displayed so that the entire shelf and step

area is filled. With whales, the step is self-contained ▲146. In some cases, where you have very large quantities of bestselling single titles either already on the table or newly arrived, put a shelf on the floor and build the display from this. The quantity of a title displayed in this manner should be sufficient to have the top of the stack at, and preferably above, the whale step height for easy shopping.

Whales can be quickly modified with removable slatwall backs and slant filler tops designed to convert the step bases into a face-up angled surface. This enhances the quality presentation of large format books in quantity.

Shelving Books on Gondolas and Whales

Merchandise presentation on gondolas and whales is as vital as it is on the front tables. The stock presentation should be maintained at the same high levels as it is in

other areas of the store. As many books as possible should always be face out, particularly hot-selling titles. Book covers have eye appeal, draw customers' attention, and stimulate customer interest. Categories within whales and gondolas should be organized in the manner that suits the particular section best. They should either be alphabetized according to author (fiction and literature), or grouped by type (cooking), subject matter (computers), or by time period (history).

Gondola merchandising starts first by adjusting shelves to provide minimum clearance for the tallest book on each shelf. Next, stock is spread evenly from bottom to top with current best-sellers and important new titles faced out for quick customer identification ▲144. After the best-sellers and new titles are faced out, continue to face out the important titles until each shelf has the maximum number of face outs with the eye-level shelves having the highest number of face outs.

With one major exception, whale merchandising follows the same procedure. Stacks of single titles are located on the two steps of the whale.

Trade and Reference Gondolas

Gondolas that contain trade hardcover titles are organized by subject with stock being evenly spread throughout the shelves and with important new titles and best-sellers faced out ▲142. To achieve this look, duplicate copies of slow-selling stock may have to be put in overstock. This may become necessary because if this gondola were filled with all the stock available, it would be totally spine out and overflowing. Extreme caution should be exercised when breaking up these titles so that sales are not lost by titles being in overstock and not on the shelf.

After the shelves are properly spaced, stock is spread evenly on all the shelves. New titles, best-sellers, and key backlist are faced out. For gondolas that have stock with similar sizes (fiction, biography), shelf spacing is very simple. In sections like sports, travel, drama, and movies, shelf spacing is difficult. Caution must be taken on the top shelf so that titles merchandised here will not obstruct the sign or fall off the side. Once the shelves are spaced, stock can be evenly placed and key titles can be faced out. If a section has several oversize titles, these can be merchandised either at the beginning or at the end of the category.

144 Above: *Local authors* are featured with New York Times best-sellers. They are discounted 30 percent and displayed face out at the store front. UNIVERSITY BOOK-STORE, Madison, Wisc.
145 Center: *Mass market best-sellers* shelved face out. A clear lucite retainer strip lists their New York Times best-seller ranking.
146 Bottom: *Bargain books* in quantity displayed on a whale fixture. B&N, New York, N.Y.

147 Top L: *Castered waterfall units* for large format children's books and furniture sets. UNIVERSITY BOOKSTORE, Madison, Wisc.
148 Top R: *Children's books.* W.A. Smith 1987, Oxford, U.K.
149 Bottom L: *All-white whale* with slatwall end-cap for children's books. UNIVERSITY BOOKSTORE, Madison, Wisc.
150 Bottom R: *Discounted bookselling* in the chain's newest store. W. A. Smith, London, U.K.

Trade and Pro-Tech Paper Gondolas

These gondolas are used for merchandising trade paper and pro-tech (professional-technical) trade reference titles. They are set up just like the hardcover gondola, starting with proper shelf spacing, even stock distribution, and key titles faced out.

NOTE: If a gondola category has a limited stock mix and title depth, it can be merchandised to create the desired image by adding key titles and facing out more secondary titles. This fills the shelves and produces the image of a well-stocked section.

Mass Market Gondolas

The gondola used for mass market titles has the same merchandising requirements as the trade hardcover and trade paper gondolas. Gondolas used to merchandise predominantly mass market stock require additional attention because of the number of titles they carry and the rapidly fluctuating title depth ▲141. To merchandise this area, start by spacing the shelves as close as possible (book height plus 1/2 inch) so that a maximum number of titles and face outs can be obtained. This is extremely important because so much of the mass market stock is trendy and impulse-oriented. Stock must be visible in order to sell. Once the shelves are spaced, distribute the stock evenly and face out key titles on every shelf. These key titles are new titles, best-sellers, backlist best-sellers, and backlist series. As stock arrives, it should be faced out on endcaps if possible ▲143. To make room for these face outs, older stock that has slowed or stopped selling should be put in overstock with one to two copies left spine out on the shelf. Occasionally, there are several trade paperbacks that cannot be merchandised in their logical order because of their size. When this occurs, place the titles on the top shelf.

151 Right: *Art and large format gondola merchandising*. PSS Bookstore, Yokosuka, Japan.

152 Below: *Art and photography books* are merchandised in this folding ladder island unit. This unit is ideal for face-out display of large calendars and coffee table books. Webster Books, Ann Arbor, Mich.

Art, Large Format, and Ladder Gondolas

Merchandising starts by first adjusting shelves to provide minimum clearance for the tallest book on each shelf. If the section has a limited number of oversize titles, these should be placed at the beginning or end of the section. Next, stock is spread evenly from bottom to top with current best-sellers and important new titles faced out for quick customer identification ▲151

After the art best-sellers and new titles are faced out, continue to face out less important titles until each shelf has the maximum number of stock in place. Folding ladder displays provide space for the seasonal expansion of art, photography, and calendar remainders ▲169. The shelves at eye level should have the highest number of face-out titles. For gondola sections with an extremely large quantity of stock, select slow-selling titles should be removed, leaving one or two

153 Top: ***Waterfall inserts*** *in children's book gondola. Plush item characters add sparkle to this display.* Bollingers Books, Oklahoma City, Okla.

154 Center: ***Well signed tables stocked*** *with face-up, spine-out bargain books in a key, first floor, high-traffic location.* Harvard Bookstore, Cambridge, Mass.

155 Bottom: ***Signs above rimmed-top tables*** *in bargain book department are hung on chains.* Charlesbank Books & Café, Boston, Mass. ▲32.

copies spine out and placing the rest into the appropriate overstock. This will create space for best-sellers and important titles to be faced out.

NOTE: Caution should be exercised on titles taken out so that sales are not lost by stock being in overstock and not on the shelf.

For gondola sections with limited stock, distribute books and face outs evenly on every shelf to fill up the section.

A limited number of gondola sections will contain oversize (large format) hard and soft bound editions of art, business, travel, decorating, cooking, trade paper, pro-tech, and mass market titles on a particular subject side by side. Strong customer interest and impact would be lost if they were displayed in two separate areas.

Crossword Puzzles, Clip Art, Music, and Activity Book Gondolas

These important categories each require face-out display. The fronts of many of these titles must be seen to be selected by customers. Inserts similar to those used for folded maps allow the flexibility of moving these categories to various locations within the store.

156 Above L: ***Crossword puzzles*** *in face-out waterfall insert.* Webster Books, Ann Arbor, Mich.
157 Above R: ***Rocking chairs for grandparents****, children's chairs, and a locomotive that kids can climb aboard (which also displays hot titles) combine with open, storytelling space in a winning arrangement.* UBS Kids, Madison, Wisc.

Bargain Books

Bargain books are a totally unique concept in the store because they offer customers the opportunity to purchase books at bargain prices. Today, most established booksellers are often able to obtain titles at greatly reduced prices. These titles may not be available anywhere else. The opportunity for a real bargain creates excitement and brings customers back again and again to check out the bargains. Bargain books may be remainder books, damaged books, used books, or special reprints of classics.

To make this part of the store exciting, it is important to follow certain steps. First, the area must stand out by grouping tables or whales in a well-defined, easily seen area at the front of the store. Second, special signing and large, bright price stickers should be used to highlight the titles. Third, tabletop display construction is geared to show titles in mass. This display construction is important because stock levels will fluctuate throughout the year and dictate the need for flexibility. When stock levels are high, more space can be given to bargain books. When stocks start to decline, space is contracted. This expansion and contraction keeps the bargain area looking full all the time, which is a key factor to maintaining the store's image.

To set up a typical bargain table book department, start first with the backmost table designated for bargain books and work toward the front of the store. This is done because the last table should be the highest, with the middle tables a little lower, and the frontmost tables, lower still. This sloping forward of the display allows the approaching customer to see all the tables at once which greatly intensifies the visual impact of the bargain book area. Two important considerations must be taken into account when merchandising the last table. When stock levels are high, the center stack of titles should not be more than 30 inches above the table ▲154. Stacks any higher than this prevent the normal customer from easy browsing, and visually blocks out the fixture or display behind them. Duplicate stock can be put in overstock. When stock levels are low, the desired height can be attained by using stacker boxes on the tables and building from them. Height is generally not a problem for whales. They can go up to seven feet high!

Building techniques for arranging the display of bargain books on whales and tables are very similar. The displays are built by positioning the most aggressively purchased titles in the center of the display. Titles are placed horizontally on the front step and vertical shelves of the whale with dust jacket facing front and sloping down on both sides. The next horizontal row on both sides of the center row are stepped down from it and the

158 Above: ***Cubes and pedestals*** *arranged in a grouping display of boxed games, and bound books.* Learningsmith, Cambridge, Mass.

159 Below: ***Painted foam core leaves*** *hang above book boxes covered with gift wrap papers to raise up toy and doll display.* GIFT SHOP, Westwood, N.J.

160 Above: ***Set of four nesting cubes*** *faced with lattice trim.* (See note 1, page 127.)

161 Below: ***Round, hexagonal, and square cubes*** *are available in custom and standard sizes and colors.* (See note 1, page 127.)

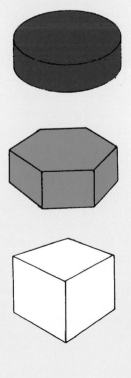

same is done for the remaining rows until the front and back edges of the table are reached. Titles are now faced out on the center row by using book rests. Titles on the next front row are faced out by propping them against the center row. Be careful not to obscure titles when facing out the lower rows. In this type of display, try to face out about 30 percent of your titles on tables, and 100 percent on whales.

Simple, direct message signing is essential to the sale of bargain books. Hanging signs and banners work just as well. When hanging your bargain books sign up, look at it from the point of view of the customer passing your store. Does it attract attention? Does it bring customers into your store? These signs are placed in the center of the middle row. They must relate to the type of bargain book on the table. Books that are true "sale" books must have a sign that tells this. Books that are remainders and reprints must have the appropriate sign. The department sign must be over the center table. Stores with two sale tables can put the sign in the middle between the two tables and high enough so that it does not obscure the table signs or interfere with customers. Once the bargain book signs are in place, care should be taken not to obscure them from the customer's view by theme signs.

Maintenance of the bargain books area is important and can be accomplished by assigning an employee to straighten it several times during the day. Stock rotation in the bargain area is also important and must be done weekly so that customers get the feeling that new, fresh stock has arrived and offers the chance to pick up a new bargain.

Used Books

The addition of used books purchased from individuals, libraries, and wholesalers to boost gross margin and hedge against competition is a growing trend. Several major chain super bookstores have added used books for the same reason. Used books are sold like remainder books with the spine up (textbook style) from tables, whales, and displayed vertically in wall shelving units. Large selections of used books are arranged by category and merchandised on rimmed sale tables with the "spine up" type of display ▲155.

Books on Tape

Most successful "books on tape" sections feature preview listening stations. Books on tape are generally packaged to resemble a quality paperback book. Audio books are easily shelved and displayed face out in tiered pocket inserts. There are several stores that specialize exclusively in the sale and rental of audio books. Achieving the right mix is no mean feat. Like everything else in the store, audio books must be seen to be sold ▲92, 162.

CD ROM

This fast-growing category is best displayed face out to maximize visibility and sales. Items may require wider shelves or waterfall type displays that are easily adapted to

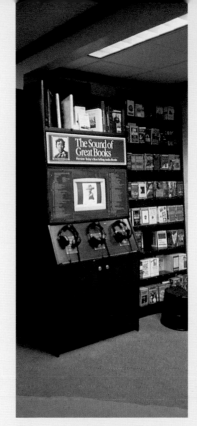

162 Above L: **Books-on-tape** *demonstration display with individual listening station.* B&N, New York, N.Y.
163 Above R: **Set of four, user-friendly, children's audio listening stations** *arranged on a slatwall-faced column. The technical image is softened with plush animals, graphics, and child-size stools.* MEDIA PLAY, Columbus, Ohio.

most store needs. Demonstration stations at the end of a gondola, table, or recessed into a wall case are important. Many users feel the need to preview samples and select the program that best suits their needs.

Bookmarks and Bookplates

Good-looking counter top and floor stand displays (that do not take up too much space) are furnished by bookmark publishers. Theses displays protect the merchandise and keep the display orderly and ready to sell bookmarks. Bookmarks are generally a good source of add-

on sales. Bookplates are available in a variety of designs and price ranges.

Boxed Sets

Boxed sets and multiple title packs paperbacks by Zane Gray and other popular authors can be ordered from publishers or shrink wrapped into sets (at the store) to make great Christmas gifts. Better boxed sets can be featured at cash and information desks on open or end-caps or in secured glass showcases. Multiple packs sell well from informal wicker baskets strategically located throughout the department in "found" space, particularly when

164 Above L: *Customer gift-wrapping station* offers a large selection of wrapping papers and ties.
165 Above R: *Coat and parcel lockers* are provided for customer convenience while shopping. Both: Hugendubel Bucher, Frankfurt, Ger.

the sets are also featured in show windows.

Calendars

Calendars are a seasonal product with a principal life span from October through January. Basic calendar display presentation can be on tables, steps, folding ladder displays, screens, wire grids, slatwall, and whales. Tabletop display construction is in a pyramid fashion with the bestselling calendar forming the pyramid peak and with lesser known calendars around each side. The top-selling calendars are to be faced out toward the store front using either large book props, easels, or cubes to lean against. The remaining stock on the table is stacked in a flat-out display.

There are other ways to handle calendars. One is to send slow-moving wall or gondola stock to overstock. The released space is then converted for the display of calendars. A favorite European technique is to hang calendars on wire grid panels in freestanding arrangements around columns, on vacant end panels, T-walls, and wall sections. Large calendars generally sell well when displayed on folding ladder type displays ▲169. Because calendars are seasonal and have a very short life after Christmas, it is important to sell as many titles as possible before Christmas. This can be accomplished by constantly restocking and by redisplaying the area daily. Calendars are a highly browsed area and as

such need constant attention and arranging. You will need to assign one or more people to watch this area and to make necessary display changes throughout the day.

Gifts and Bookends

Many bookstores owe their success to the successful merchandising of both gifts and books. The ratio of one product assortment to the other varies. The variety of gifts ranges even further. Institutional stores located in art or history museums, or at national parks feature gifts and books that relate to their own and to other museum collections. They also feature items relating to their geographic location and the image of the insti-

tution. Gifts range from post cards, key chains, bookends, blank books, maps, special interest books, mini-books, prints, posters, plush to Waterford crystal, and fine jewelry. It is crucial to understand the concept that customers buy for price, image, and nostalgia. For this reason your product assortment must reflect your store's image. If you intend to really merchandise gifts it will be well to consider providing wrapping and shipping service.

Globes

Globes of all types add to the ambiance of the store. They can be displayed on ledges, tables, gondolas, stands, and racks supplied by vendors. Most DVM

166 Above: *City, state, country, world maps, and globes* are combined in this compact map shop. Charlesbank Books & Cafe, Boston, Mass.
167 Below: *A three dimensional globe is mounted* to a slatwall panel as a multilingual prop in this travel department—a great idea! Airport Shop, Charlotte, N.C.

168 Above: *The imaginative use of slatwall shelves,* wire baskets, and card holders make this tiny greeting card and gift wrap section a huge success. WORDSWORTH ABRIDGED, Cambridge, Mass. 169 Below: *Folding ladder racks display a large selection of calendars in the fall.* The racks can then be used for face-out display of large format books and remainders. BookPeople Bookstore & Café, Austin, Tex.

are needed to accommodate the size of various state, city and wall maps. Rolled maps can be merchandised in special box holders or in wicker baskets. Large topographical maps are best housed in large architectural type flat files. Small 8-1/2 inch by 11 inch study maps (used in school work) are often stored in suspension files of cabinets located in the department. They need to be readily available for customers to browse through.

Greeting Cards and Gift Wraps

Super high-volume sales can be generated in a small space with the right mix of card designs and wraps. Cards and wraps can be made to work well when the majority of the end-caps of a store are committed to their presentation. High card and wrap sales volume can be generated with acrylic tiered pocket wall displays located in compact niches and alcove display settings ▲168. Full line card and wrap stores are another story.

Picture and Post Cards

For the most part DVM people like to market these products in acrylic trays. They are often mounted in slatwall tracks, on gondola end-caps ▲125, and on attractive revolving spinner displays. The advantage is that the full face of the design is in view. Revolving floor stands on casters that can be moved easily are handy in stores selling a lot of this product.

people prefer to display lighted globes side by side with tabletop globes. They can also be displayed on wall ledges, on the top of closed-top gondolas and on tables. Various models of floor globes in a wide price range sell well when positioned in the travel department on carpeted floors next to map displays. This is convenient for customers and it makes sense.

Maps ▲166

Maps must be organized for customers to find the one they need. Maps are best merchandised in slotted pocket display inserts. Several sizes of inserts

Store fixtures located in the front and center
of the store "sell" the image of the store
and the products on display.

The interior of a store and its visual presentation
is a statement of what booksellers
want the public to think of the store.

Customers expect to find new-arrival theme
and sale tables full and well merchandised
at the front of the store.

New-arrival wall cases are popular in small stores.

Whales are versatile, new, high-capacity sales fixtures
that combine traditional step displays with face-out
shelving capability and are ideal for new arrivals,
sale, and remainder books.

Gondola merchandising starts first by adjusting
shelves to provide minimum clearance for
the tallest book on each shelf.

Use gondola end-caps to
reemphasize bestselling titles.

★ ★ ★ ★ ★

Graphics and Improvisation

8

Subtle changes in the design of merchandising and promotional signs are taking place in independent bookstores. What kind of graphics do we see? The changes are the quick-read, easily understood, meaningful messages and brighter colors and bolder letter styles that are pictured in this chapter. These visual images are being integrated into the store's logo. Image plans are slowly being adjusted to appeal more directly to the demographics of the store's customer base.

Banners and Signs

There is a continuing trend toward the use of simple and well-designed hanging banner type signs. Banners can be as simple as messages developed on a desktop PC and reproduced on a color copier. The final product can be inserted into an acrylic banner type holder or applied to foam core boards and hung from the ceiling on filament line or acrylic chain ▲67. Banners produced in-store can also be applied to a thin painted piece of acrylic material or applied to sturdy art papers suspended from the ceiling ▲170.

Banner stands are available in table top and floor versions ▲32. They bring a fresh, flexible approach for stores to target specific messages more closely.

Electronic Information Technology and Directories

CD ROM-based information technology terminals supplement good, basic, category, regional signage, directory, and other information devices. These terminals are adaptable to most retail bookstore environments. Customers can preview samples of 30 or more of the latest audio books or listen to up to 500 samples from 150 albums, from Pearl Jam to Chopin music selections. Mind-boggling music databases with over one million song titles and 130,000 album titles are precisely categorized by musical genre. Classical works are arranged according to composers. Supplementary information regarding labels, catalog numbers, and UPC codes are provided. Video databases include over 50,000 movie titles, including closed-captioned, laser disk, education, and general interest categories. All it takes is money. Not every bookstore is expected to provide these electronic marvels, but booksellers are expected to know and understand these developments and decide which of these devices will provide the most effective image-building service to their customers.

170 Left: ***Total, yet controlled, improvisation*** *captures children's and parents' imagination through the use of promotional posters on a clothesline, a chest for eclectic fixturing, T-walls, an open-leg sale table, floor stands, and flying characters.* HICKELBEES,' San Jose, Calif.

Author Signing

171 Below: ***Author signings and discussions*** *are important in-store marketing events requiring innovative, improvised solutions. Round-table discussions, cooking, art, craft, and film demonstration events are common in larger stores.*

Author Presentation

172 Below: ***Audience seated on 50 folded chairs*** *located in the main aisle after the tables have been cleared.* Libertie's Books & Music, Boca Raton, Fla.

Store coordinator   Signing

Customer   Books to be signed   Author   Samples

Low table   Books to be signed   Authors chair   Podium   Author

Author Discussion

173 Left: ***Sale and theme tables*** *are rolled to other locations in the basement level to accommodate author discussion, and question/answer session.* STACEY'S, San Francisco, Calif.

Author Presentation

174 Left: ***Large first floor area*** *is devoted to audience seating for author discussion. Space is found by moving sale and theme tables. Folding chairs are stored in the back rooms.* Kepler's Books & Magazines, Menlo Park, Calif.

175 Above L: ***Innovative use of garage door*** *for a no-frills store front.*
176 Above R: ***A festive, summertime atmosphere*** *at a Saturday afternoon gathering.* Both: Learningsmith, Cambridge, Mass.
177 Center: ***A tent sale*** *in the yard of a strip center.* More Good Books, Southbury, Conn.
178 Below: ***Outdoor bookselling.*** Frankfurt Book Fair, Frankfurt, Ger.

179-180 Above L, R: *Two of the first displays promoting discount book prices* following the abolishment of the net book-pricing agreement in Britan. W.A. Smith, Sloan Square 1995, London, U.K.
181 Below L: *Slatwall faced column merchandising* in a children's book department. WORDSWORTH, Cambridge, Mass.
182 Below R: *Adjustable cross bars with display hooks* (attached to the face of a column) are used to merchandise custom design tote bags and hang up items. Metropolitan Opera Gift Shop, New York, N.Y.

183 Above L: *Attractive lighted signs in store* outlines the entrance of the children's department.
184 Above R: *A quality curb sign* designed to appeal to students and faculty alike is located in an interior concourse to mark the main entrance of the store. Minnesota Book Center, Minneapolis, Minn.
185 Below: *The bright colors* and aggressive graphics used in this lively New York City classical music department visually arrest the customers curiosity. 186 Bottom: *Bright, exposed fluorescent and neon lights* and competing graphic styles in the signage are combined to establish the visual tone and price awareness atmosphere of this successful super-discount music store. Both: Tower Records, New York, N.Y.

187 Left: *This beautifully designed exterior sign* conveys an image of quality and commitment to service. The Book Collector, Houston, Tex.

188 Below L: *A friendly curb sign* is wheeled out each day to attract the attention of heavy street traffic passing by. The Book Collector, Houston, Tex.

189 Below R: *A neat curb sign* with a clear, easily understood service message. Disneyworld. Buena Vista, Fla.

OPPOSITE PAGE

190 Top L: *Adhesive faced vinyl letters* are applied to the show window glass to state a seasonal sales message. The use of white letters on window glass is a popular choice among booksellers. KATE'S, New York, N.Y.

191 Center L: *The major book departments* in the store are listed on a color coordinated directory built around an exterior column at the entrance of. ..Hugendubel Bucher, Frankfurt, Ger.

192 Center R: *The entrance to Hugendubel Bucher,* the busy German superstore. Hugendubel Bucher, Frankfurt, Ger.

193 Bottom R: *Expensive, but classy lighted signs.* DILLON'S, London, U.K.

Curb Signs

A good idea coming back into use again is curb signs. Curb signs are attention-grabbing devices designed to turn pedestrian street traffic into store traffic ▲184, 188.

For years independent bookstores have turned to portable signs, easily positioned by the curb, in parking lots, and at the door to provide a versatile method for getting their message to the public ▲189. Now that they have returned, they seem to be more

194 Above: *Children relax on bean bags while watching a video screen recessed into the wall at their eye level.* MEDIA PLAY, Columbus, Ohio.
195 Below: *Seated by a working fireplace, Lee Bollinger* browses through one of the thousands of titles stocked by...Bollingers Books, Oklahoma City, Okla.

experience of what the store stands for to be better on a day-by-day basis than its competition. DVM is a strategy to create a competitive advantage. It is one reason some major superstores pursue it so vigorously.

Retail stores that reach out spasmodically with DVM presentations are not as successful as those who regularly pursue it with passion. To take advantage of new opportunities, a bookstore must pursue a no-nonsense systematic approach to implementing DVM strategy. It must be the first order of business for a store moving into the future.

Improvised Events

All bookstores are, at one time or another, invited to participate in some kind of in-store or off-site book fair. When it is warranted, DVM techniques can add style to the happening. This is done by providing easels, table-cloths (with big store logo), store bags, brochures, catalogs, and bookmarks to turn the book fair

buying experience into a gratifying shopping experience—an extension of the main store image.

Appearances by authors for autograph sessions in the store may be one or more individuals, a writing team, or a musical group.

There are many reasons why the appearance of a popular or newsworthy author willing to give a talk, do a reading, and sign copies of a new book are important to a bookstore and worth the extra effort to set up, promote, and accommodate the writer.

Have a guest register available for each author to sign and hopefully write a message of his/her impressions of your store for future promotion. Signings can be a wonderful strategy for reaching out to the community to attract more customers into the store. It keeps your store close to your customers ▲171.

Demonstrations

In-store demonstrations are really another personal selling

popular than ever. Where local ordinances permit, these distinctive curb signs have proven to be an effective, economical promotional vehicle.

Improvisation

Improvisation in a retail bookstore applies techniques to personalize the image of the store and meet the expectations of its clientele. Customers expect the technique. Demonstrations which are of benefit to your customers can be used to attract prospective book buyers to share in a learning or entertainment experience. Customers enjoy watching and participating in cooking, science exhibits, children's school exhibits, magic, card games, Easter egg coloring, drawing, painting, sewing, hiking, kite making, and dozens of other interactive in-store demonstrations. They will talk about them with their neighbors. Demonstrations targeted to specific market categories can attract many different audiences, and help build your repeat customer base. Just think of the excitement and business you can generate with in-store demonstrations.

Subtle changes in the design of point-of-purchase signs are taking place in all types of stores.

More emphasis is placed on creating better night image with light.

All types of banner signs and holders are gaining favor as image-building devices as well as points of information.

CD ROM-based information technology is here to stay.

Curb signs have made a comeback.

Improvisation is relied upon more and more to accommodate in-store events.

Bookfairs, author appearances, story telling, demonstrations, lectures, and music programs are a few of the important promotional elements that contribute to the visual force that brings the customers and stores together in today's competitive environment.

★ ★ ★ ★ ★

DVM is the visual sum of merchandising a business. It is a reflection of a store's level of imagination. It is a product of the store's personality. It is the basic tool to reengineer your store. DVM is a tool that can bring the store and customer together...and, this is by no means an overstatement!

INDEX

CREDITS

PHOTOGRAPHY CREDITS

The author and the publisher would like to thank the many booksellers whose stores are featured in this book. Every effort has been made to obtain the names of photographers and copyright clearance. We do apologize if any omissions have been made. Any credits due that are brought to the publisher's attention will be credited in the next printing.

The following credits are in numerical order of the photo as they appear on the pages of the book. Ken White is identified as KW, Paul Marsh as PM, Bill Mitchell as BM, Herb Nelson as HN, Sherri Svekas as SS, and Peter Smokowski as PS.

1–13 KW; 14–16 PM; 17–20 KW; 21 PM; 22 KW; 23, 24 PM; 25, 26 KW; 27–29 PM; 30–34 KW; 35–39 PM; 40, 41 KW; 42 PM; 43–50 KW; 51–53 PM; 55–59 KW; 60 PM; 61-78 KW, 79 PM; 80-82 KW; 83, 84 PM; 85–87; 88–90 PM; 91–96 KW; 97,98 PM; 99 KW; 100 BM; 102, PM;103–105 KW; 107 PM; 108 HN; 109–112 KW; 113, 114 PM; 117, 118 KW; 119–121 PM; 122–126 KW; 127 PM; 129 HN; 130-133 PM; 134, 135 KW; 137 PM; 138, 139 KW; 141–143 KW; 144 HN; 144-145 PM; 147-154 KW; 155 BM; 156, 157 HN; 158–160 KW; 163 PM; 164, 165 KW; 166 BM; 167-170 KW; 171, 172 SS; 173–184 KW; 185, 186 PM; 187–192 KW; 193 PS; 194 PM; 195 KW.

ARCHITECTURAL CREDITS

Bookstores which appear and that were designed by others include:

Airport Shops Detroit, Atlanta, Charlotte, San Francisco, B&N; BOOKS-A-MILLION; Bookshop, Santa Cruz; Borders Books and Music; DILLON'S; Golden Bookshop; Harry W. Schwartz; Harvard Bookstore; Hugendubel Bucher; HICKELBEES;' Kaiser Buchhandlung; Kepler's Books & Magazines; KATE'S; Learningsmith; MEDIA PLAY; More Good Books; Noodle Kidoodle; Phileas Fogg's Books & More; Sam Goody's; Scribner; Shakespear & Co.; Sloan Square 1995; STACEY'S; Tattered Cover Bookstore; Tower Records; UBS Kids; Comic Store Universal Walk; UNIVERSITY BOOKSTORE; UPSTART CROW BOOKSTORE; W.A. Smith, London, Oxford; WATERSTONES Booksellers; WordsWorth, WORDSWORTH ABRIDGED; ZANY BRAINY

ENDNOTES

1. Source for props: TRIMCO, 459 W. 15th Street, New York, N.Y. 10011; Tel. (212) 989-1616, Fax (212) 243-6138

2. Watch furniture clearance sales for room furnishings such as lawn, beach, occasional furniture, lamps, shades, curtains, and drapery.

3. Fully dimensional, six piece book sets ranging in size from 8 by 11 inch to 16 by 24-inch. They are available in either plaid or solid covers. Subject titles include history, geography, biology, math, English and music.

4. The basic color of the baker's rack is black with brass appointments. Additional colors are available. Inquire directly to TRIMCO.

MORE ANSWERS TO YOUR QUESTIONS

International Display and Visual Merchandising Advice For You Worldwide by Fax, Telephone, or Internet E-mail.

After you have read this book, have applied what you've learned to your business, and have thought about the whole matter for awhile, you may still have questions.

To get answers to specific questions on a paid basis, you can contact Ken White worldwide by phone or fax for a consultation. Rates are U.S. $90 for a half hour, and U.S. $180 for one hour which are comparable to attorney fees.

In order for you to gain the most from this type of strategic business consultation while keeping your costs to a minimum, please follow this procedure:

1. Contact Ken White by fax at (201) 664-0750, by phone at (201) 664-5664, or by E-mail at KWHITECONS@AOL.COM
2. Leave your name, the type of business you own or operate, and the exact time you can be called back over the next several days.
3. Expect to receive a collect call at that time.

Ken will return your call, listen to your questions, and then advise you whether one-on-one telephone consultation would be appropriate for your situation. If the answer is yes, you will be asked to pick a time for the phone consultation, normally within two weeks, and you will be told the cost of the consultation.

If you are faced with a crisis, a "quick response" schedule may be possible. At this time, Ken will send you a briefing questionnaire to help expedite the consultation. You will need to send back to Ken:

1. Your completed questionnaire.
2. A description of your business including the number of employees, range of sales, years in business, location of facilities, a photograph of your store and/or the department where appropriate, and a brief summary of the questions you are asking.
3. A check for the amount of the consultation.

That's it. In most cases there should be little problem in doing the rest by phone or by fax. Ken White has joined in strategic partnering and consulting with over eight hundred clients in his forty-year career. He has established the leading reputation for doing what he says he will do — and more. If he can help, he will, if he can't, he'll say so.

Your guarantee is that if you are not satisfied that the consultation was worth the price of Ken's time and the long-distance charges, send him a letter explaining why you are not satisfied and half of your consulting fee will be refunded with no questions asked. You must make this request within one week of the consultation.

Ken White designed this new service to offer independent booksellers and their advisors a fresh, outside perspective filled with creditable ideas that warrant careful attention and are capable of immediate translation. It is a new effort to put all of the innovative ideas, skill, and resources associated with world-class consulting at your disposal.